WE NEED EACH OTHER

To Transform America

The Call for Unity to
Solve Our National Problems Together

Reginald F. Davis, Ph.D.

SCRIPTORIA

an imprint of Sunbury Press, Inc.
Mechanicsburg, PA USA

an imprint of Sunbury Press, Inc.
Mechanicsburg, PA USA

For information about special discounts for bulk purchases, please contact Sunbury Press Orders Dept. at (855) 338-8359 or orders@sunburypress.com.

To request one of our authors for speaking engagements or book signings, please contact Sunbury Press Publicity Dept. at publicity@sunburypress.com.

FIRST SCRIPTORIA PRESS EDITION: May 2025

Set in Adobe Garamond | Interior design by Crystal Devine | Cover by Lawrence Knorr | Edited by Lawrence Knorr.

Publisher's Cataloging-in-Publication Data
Names: Davis, Reginald F., author.
Title: We need each other to transform America : the call for unity to solve our national problems together / Reginald F. Davis, Ph.D.
Description: First trade paperback edition. | Mechanicsburg, PA : Scriptoria Press, 2025.
Summary: Out of love for America and the hunger found among different races, faiths, and political parties, who desire to bridge the divide in our nation, there is hope that we can achieve national unity to solve our national problems if we return to God, our core values, and treat one another as citizens and not as enemies.
Identifiers: ISBN 979-8-88819-347-1 (softcover).
Subjects: RELIGION / Christian Education / Children & Youth | RELIGION / Christian Ministry / Youth | RELIGION / Christian Living / Personal Growth.

Designed in the USA
0 1 1 2 3 5 8 13 21 34 55

For the Love of Books!

To the American citizens who are working and
dedicated to building one nation, under God,
indivisible with liberty and justice for all.

We need to keep our eyes on the mission and realize that we need each other if we're going to pull this off. . . . The early church produced the book of Acts; the modern church produced a book of Talks. Their leaders died living out the gospel; we make a living by talking about it. The more we bear fruit, the easier unity will be.

—FRANCIS CHAN

CONTENTS

ACKNOWLEDGMENTS

I would like to acknowledge my wife, Myrlene, and family for their encouragement and support. I would like to thank Clifton Brigham and the Williamsburg community for their support. Also, I want to thank Dr. Lawrence Knorr, Crystal Devine, and the Sunbury Press staff for their kindness, professionalism, and support in publishing this work.

FOREWORD

I first met Dr. Reginald Davis when he preached years ago at the church I attend. In his sermon he talked about how the black church and the white church were better together, that we need each other. Since that meeting our relationship has grown into a precious friendship. Dr. Davis's heart for unity as well as for justice and freedom, has challenged and inspired me. As a white Christian, I didn't know what I didn't know. Through many times of fellowship over meals, shared stories and conversations, I have learned so much from him. I have "new eyes" as I view the current racial situation and Church division in our nation. Our greater Williamsburg community is so fortunate and blessed to have Dr. Davis as a leader. He is always looking for ways to build bridges and encourage oneness and create opportunities for unity and better understanding. I believe this book is another step in accomplishing these goals.

Dr. Davis is a gifted communicator, speaking from decades of experience. In this book he is calling us to fulfil the original intent of our nation's founding documents, of liberty and justice for all. In the following pages, he eloquently lays out the problems our country currently faces regarding, race, injustice, and disunity, and offers practical solutions. In each chapter you will find hope for the future. Dr. Davis is calling us to a higher standard and he makes it clear that we can't do this alone. Everyone must do their part, and with God's help, this can be accomplished. There is hope through the efforts of a united Church.

We are still a deeply divided country. Dr. Davis shows that though we may not feel it is our fault, or our problem, it is our responsibility. The reason we have this problem of racial division and disunity, is that in the past, many in the Church did not seriously address it, and if we do not take responsibility, we will leave this problem to our children and grandchildren.

We cannot have change without trust. We cannot have trust without relationships, and we cannot have relationships without conversations. This book calls us to sit down and talk to one another instead of shouting at each other or just ignoring one other. Reconciliation means creating new relationships, new friendships. As Dr. Davis emphasizes, this is not easy to accomplish. It will take trust, understanding, and repentance, before we achieve true unity. He challenges the leaders in our cities, to always be ready to step in to advance unity through words and actions to address the needs of the city and bring about the healing of the divisions that have separated us for too long.

There are at least three steps to solving a problem. First there must be agreement that there IS a problem. Next there must be agreement about what that problem is, and finally there must be agreement on how to fix the problem, before we can ever hope to begin to solve the problem. In this book, Dr. Davis gives us a road map to accomplish these steps.

In the Bible's book of Luke, we read the story of Jesus raising Lazurus from the dead. Many people today are praying for a resurrection, a miracle in our country, but I believe we miss a key part of the story. Before Jesus raised Lazurus, something very important first had to happen. The stone needed to be removed. A detail rarely talked about is that Jesus did not remove the stone. His followers removed it. Could it be that we are asking God to come and heal our land, to bring resurrection life and racial healing to our nation, but God is waiting for us to first remove the stone? We can do this through acknowledging the oppressions and injustices of the past, through lament and repentance and reconciliation.

Could it be that we are waiting on God to act but He is waiting on us? God has told us what to do. Dr. Davis is calling us to roll the stone so that God can bring the healing and fulfil the great promises and purposes of our nation. As he states in the following pages, America must first take ownership of the true fulfillment of our founding documents granting liberty and justice for all.

This book is a clarion call to get involved. The Church needs to wake up and step into this problem together. Dr. Davis points out that the cancer of division is eating away at our republic. We cannot expect unity within the nation when there is no unity within the Church. Too many Christians are sitting on the sidelines. We need to be intentional about working together. We have the skill and knowledge required to complete this task, but do we lack the will? The Church must stop emphasizing its differences and concentrate on its commonality. What affects one of us affects us all. So as Dr. Davis makes so clear, cooperation is essential in the quest for transformation. We must bear one another's burdens. Our future is contingent upon us realizing how much we "need each other."

—CLIFTON L. BRIGHAM, CPA, MST

Founder and retired partner of Brigham, Calhoun, Whitson & Associates, PC.
A leader of Greater Williamsburg Movement that seeks to bring transformation to the City through the unity of the Church, to see our cities experience the spiritual and social flourishing God has laid out in His Word.

INTRODUCTION

Years ago, I was invited to a white congregation to help forge racial unity in the community and hopefully produce unity throughout the nation. The message I preached was called, "We need each other." This message resonated with many people, and years later people are still saying how this message needs to get out across the country. Upon constant affirmation of the message, I decided to put this message in a much broader context to reach others across the nation who have a deep yearning for national unity. Deep down inside of us, we resent the division, crime, and ugliness we see in our nation that threatens our future. Regardless of our differences, we are all connected in one way or another. To be human is to yearn to be connected to other humans. The Creator made us this way, and this yearning to be connected will forever be within our souls.

We see this with children who come from different parts of the world, and somehow, they want to play with one another despite their racial, religious, and cultural differences. They are drawn to one another because not only are they humans but social beings as well. Countless humans may not admit it, but we are all creations of God wherever we are located on this planet, and we need each other to realize our commonality. All humans need oxygen to breathe, water to drink, food to survive, a community to connect with, and purpose to accomplish things together. If any of these things go lacking, we won't survive long on this planet. Therefore, we need each other to survive and thrive in life.

Since God is our Creator, God is also the Great Synthesizer to bring together disconnected humanity into a harmonious whole. Due to the fall of humanity and its separation from God, humanity has been divided from itself. This division is still an ongoing saga, causing humanity to experience a living hell on earth. Until humanity reconnects with God and one another, this living hell continues unabated. To transform America, we need to be more loving, just, and empathic towards one another and intentional about working together in unity. Unity does not mean uniformity. In other words, we won't agree all the time, but disagreement should not lead to being disagreeable.

Having different perspectives and different experiences should be welcomed because transforming America takes bringing together differences to create solutions for complicated problems. We live in a complicated world with complicated problems. We were all born in this complicated world and inherited its consequences. Meshed between this complicated world is our conscience, and if we set our hearts and minds on conscience, we can achieve solutions that benefit all and not just a privileged few. Our world is in a mess because the ultra-rich are controlling the decisions of the nation, creating conditions that are tearing apart the nation and the world. We can no longer sit back and allow a few to make decisions for the many. We can no longer accept the rich getting richer while the rest of us are barely making ends meet. Union workers are beginning to strike again to bring attention to the inequities that exist in the nation. Workers are only asking for a fair share of the profits to not only purchase the products they make but also to provide a better future for their children. The American dream should not only be for those at the top of the economic heap but also for those who want a fair share of the American dream as well. To achieve fairness and justice, we have to involve ourselves in the decisions and direction of the nation and hopefully snatch it back from those who are ruining its possible future. "When Americans insisted, with one voice, that labor was the source of all value, they were not simply repeating a theoretical truism. The labor theory of value was more than an abstract principle of political economy in a country where labor's contribution to the general well-being took the form of mind as well as muscle."[1] To save our democracy, we must speak and act with one voice again.

1. Christopher Lasch, *The Revolt of the Elite and the Betrayal of Democracy* (New York: W.W. Norton & Company, 1995), 60.

In addition to acting and speaking with one voice, we must believe that our nation and planet are worth saving. Our Creator put under our authority the ability to save ourselves and the planet from destruction. The transformation of our nation is not God's responsibility but ours. People ask, "Why doesn't God stop the war? Why doesn't God stop hunger? Why doesn't God stop the destruction of humanity? Why doesn't God stop racism and social and economic inequities?" The answer is God didn't start these things. God didn't draft policies that give luxuries to the few at the expense of the many. God didn't create events that leave millions of humans homeless, starving, sick, and disease-ridden. God didn't create weapons of mass destruction, nor does He approve of them being used on other human beings. Humans create the problems we face, and therefore, humans must solve them. God respects our decisions, and when humans make destructive decisions, God will not intervene to do for humans what they collectively must do for themselves. God is an ally in the struggle to transform America and the world, but God will not overrule divine law and intervene in the affairs of mankind at points of His displeasure. To sit back and allow a few to rob, steal, and destroy what belongs to all of us is a testament and travesty to how far we have fallen as humans and how spiritually and intellectually undeveloped we have become. This is the reason cooperation is essential in the quest for transformation. A willingness to work together with the realization that we need each other leads to the transformation of our nation.

When people of goodwill put their hearts and minds together, they can achieve the impossible. Look how President John F. Kennedy challenged us to reach the moon, and in less than a decade, we put men and women on the moon. With international cooperation, we have built an international space station and can see untold galaxies and planets throughout the universe. Now, if human ingenuity can build a space station with international cooperation, human ingenuity can equally solve problems facing us today. Over the years, we have fed millions who are hungry; we have housed millions without shelter; we have formed international alliances to stop madmen like Hitler and Mussolini with their dangerous ideologies from taking over the world. We have passed legislation to include several people to have life, liberty, and access to opportunities. We have extended healthcare to many and started many organizations to help the disadvantaged and the displaced. There is no question that during the last 100 years, we faced complicated problems, and with collective efforts solved these complicated problems for the benefit of mankind. We have come a long way in the last 100 years, and who's to say we won't make much more progress in the years to come? Our future is contingent upon us realizing how we need each other.

Our nation and the world are in such tremendous trouble that if we don't realize we need each other, the world is doomed. How is it when a natural disaster happens like an earthquake or hurricane, we forget, if only temporarily, about race, religion, culture, and politics and face our common problems together for the sake of the community? Does it take disaster after disaster for us to see that we need each other? Does it take nature to remind us that we cannot make it alone in this world? Maya Angelou said, "We are obliged to know we are global citizens. Disasters remind us we are world citizens, whether we like it or not."[2] Just like we pull together across racial, cultural, and political lines during natural disasters, it ought to be a common practice to solve critical problems facing us today. There is no doubt when we all lean in with our gifts and talents with hearts generated by love, no problem can go unsolved. We all carry within us solutions to human problems when we realize we need each other. If we can ever look past our differences, see each other as human beings and allow ourselves to bring to bear our different contributions to solve problems, we can transform America. When situations and circumstances are transformed, the credit goes to all of us. We all benefit from the transformation. If there is a concern about who gets the credit, let us agree that we all get it for our cooperation. When we become mature enough to remove the "I" for the "We," the transformation of our nation is within reach.

I am writing this book because I believe in the human potential to transform America and the world. There are more people than problems, and when each person takes it upon him or herself to be a part of the solution, there isn't anything we cannot solve. We must first find common ground and begin the work of transformation. We all see life from different perspectives and have different experiences. The common ground is to listen to one another, agree on core values as a nation, and find intersections

2. Maya Angelou, "Brainy Quotes," brainyquote.com

where we can connect and work to transform our nation by bringing it in line with its established creeds. One thing is sure: if the nation falls, we fall with it regardless of race, nationality, political party, and socioeconomic position. Martin Luther King, Jr. called it our "Inescapable network of mutuality, tied in a single garment of destiny."[3] The brokenness in our nation can be mended, and the sickness can be healed. Our problem is not only physical, emotional and psychological; it is mainly spiritual. Our hearts and minds need spiritual healing, and when we neglect spiritual healing, the physical and all it entails cannot be made whole.

God has given mankind the authority on earth, and we have a responsibility before God to solve human problems. We have solved human problems before, and we can solve them again. The collective work of countless people has led to significant changes which have impacted lives around the world. There is no question we have the ingenuity but lack the will. Once our will and ingenuity link with love and justice, there is no stopping short of transformation. Together, we can strengthen our democracy and dismantle hurdles in our way. We can smooth down rough roads of opposition against egalitarianism. We can crush racism, sexism, ethnocentrism, and build bridges of opportunity for every community, and create a more just and humane society. We can disrupt the fusion of hate, bitterness, and injustice that is creating luminous darkness from sea to shining sea. The darkness is around us, but it doesn't have to be in us. Amanda Gorman stated, "There is always light if only we are brave enough to see it. If only we are brave enough to be it."[4] If there is a multi-coalition of conscience to push bipartisanship of our political leaders to work for the interest of all citizens, we could soon see glimpses of light shooting through the silhouette of this American life. Together, we can achieve educational equality and workplace justice. We can transform the criminal justice system and save our youth from the culture of violence and death. We can stop mass shootings that are abysmally out of control. We can create a comprehensive immigration policy that is just and fair. We can transform our national and international crisis once we realize we need each other to create a better and safer world.

---

3. Martin Luther King, Jr. , "Letter from the a Birmingham Jail," April 16, 1963.
4. Amanda Gorman, "The Hill We Climb," Inaugural Poem at the Presidential Inauguration, January 22, 2021.

The problems facing us are not outside the realm of human achievement. What it is going to take is faith in God, love of neighbor, love of country, humbleness, empathy, and treating people like we want to be treated. Nobody wants to be treated with injustice; nobody wants to be exploited; nobody wants to be treated like they don't matter as human beings. If we don't want to be mistreated, exploited, and mishandled, then let us make sure we don't treat others like this. What is needed in America is not retribution but love, justice, and forgiveness. Without it, our nation will drift into deeper darkness. The future of our nation is dependent upon the choices we make today. It is my hope and prayer that we choose light over darkness, life over death, unity over division, love over hate, peace over war, patriotism over partisan politics, and justice over injustice. Our human potential is greater than the problems that are destroying us. The late President Jimmy Carter stated, "The bond of our common humanity is stronger than the divisiveness of our fears and prejudices. God gives us the capacity for choice. We can choose to alleviate suffering. We can choose to work together for peace. We can make these changes—and we must."[5] It is colossally sad to see our potential wasted by our failure to see and understand that we need each other in a world that is waiting for transformation.

If America means anything, it means opportunity. We have an opportunity to transform darkness into a marvelous light of love, justice, brotherhood, and sisterhood. All it takes is for us to stop emphasizing our differences and concentrate on our commonality. When we do this, we can realize our greatest potential and achievement in the world. Let there be no doubt we have what it takes to transform America. We are not infinitely deprived of values and moral vision in an immoral world. The better angels of our nature are lying dormant within us, waiting for the right tapping. If the downward spiral of society and the nation have not created the right tapping to release the better angels of nature, I don't know what else will. But what I do know is when we allow the better angels of our nature to rise, a new world is waiting to rise. The question is, will we give ourselves a chance to create this new world? Will we humble ourselves and come together and pass on a better nation to generations to come? Howard Thurman stated, "There is a spirit in man and the world working

---

5. Jimmy Carter, Nobel Lecture, Oslo, December 10, 2002.

always against the thing that destroys and lays waste. Always he must know that the contradictions of life are not final or ultimate; he must distinguish between failure and the many-sided awareness so that he will not mistake conformity for harmony, uniformity for synthesis."[6] Once we get with the Spirit that builds up what is torn down and harmonizes what is being separated, we have a great opportunity to not only see our commonality but this commonality is our salvation. Let us not forget this very important scripture that proves we all share a common ancestry as human beings. It is found in the book of Acts 17:26 that says, "From one man [God] made all the nations, that they inhabit the whole earth; and [God] marked out their appointed times in history and the boundaries of their lands." Since God made us, it is up to us to work together to save our nation and the world.

If we truly love our nation despite its many disappointments, twists and turns, and existential threats, and it is worth transforming, then we must find a way together to save it. Psalms 133:1-3 tells us the benefit of coming together in unity. "Behold, how good and pleasant it is [for God's people] to dwell together in unity . . . It is like the dew of Hermon coming down upon the mountains of Zion; for there the Lord commanded the blessing." I hope we still believe in the words of Samuel Francis Smith:

> My country, 'tis of thee, sweet land of liberty, of thee I sing. Land where my fathers died, land of the pilgrims' pride, from every mountainside, let freedom ring . . . our fathers God, to Thee, Author of liberty, to Thee, we sing; long may our land be bright, with freedom's holy light, protect us by Thy might, Great God, our King.[7]

6. Howard Thurman, *The Search For Common Ground* (Richmond, IN: Friends United Press, 1986), 6.
7. Samuel Francis Smith, "My Country, Tis of Thee, Sweet Land of Liberty," 1832.

Chapter One

WE NEED EACH OTHER

Life doesn't make any sense without interdependence. We need each other, and the sooner we learn that, the better for us all.

—ERIK ERIKSON

"We, the people," begins the preamble to our Constitution; it is the cement of our nation and democracy. To maintain democracy means the cement must be protected by cleaning and repairing it of any grime, build-up, and cracks. Once cracks appear in the concrete, we must reseal it. Racism, injustice, inequality, violence, disunity, and political and economic recklessness are putting deeper cracks in the concrete of an already fractured structure, and pretty soon, the concrete will fail, and the structure of our republic will come tumbling down. When signs in the concrete are ignored, and there is no sense of urgency to repair the cracks, the structure eventually gives way. There are visible signs in the concrete structure of America, and it takes "We the people" to reseal the concrete of our great republic. If we truly love America and its future, we must lay aside our petty differences and collectively work together to prevent the downfall of the nation. If the nation falls, it won't matter about our differences. We all will be pinned under the rubble of a collapsed nation, trying to dig our way out of the concrete and debris of our benign neglect of what mattered: the preservation of our republic.

To prevent this from happening, we must come together with a sense of urgency and understand we are all at risk, and it's going to take us all to snatch back our nation from the brink of disaster. No one group can do all it takes to save our nation no more than it did to build our nation. There must be a shared responsibility to save the nation. There is no doubt we are stronger together than apart. To make honey takes more than one bee; to gather enough food for winter takes more than one ant; to wipe out a crop takes more than one grasshopper; to build bridges takes more than one man; to make an automobile takes more than one employee; to win a war takes one than one soldier; to win a basketball or football game takes more than one player. To advance the Kingdom of God takes more than one disciple of Jesus Christ. Whether we know it or not, we need each other more than we think. Human habitation on earth cannot survive without the cooperation of nations agreeing to come together and work against what affects us all, like war, climate change, air pollution, pandemics, and social and economic injustice, just to name a few. Shawn McAndrew cogently stated:

> No matter how much someone may irritate you, or trigger negative patterns, there's usually an opportunity for awareness, shift, enlightenment, to let go. As humans, we always have the choice to learn something from others. Opening our hearts to those we may not agree with politically, theoretically, religiously, or fundamentally allows us to widen our knowledge . . . . If we close ourselves off from people who don't think like we do, vote like we do, or pray like we do, we stunt our growth and suffocate our minds. We are, after all, spiritual beings having a human experience. The spirit in every person we encounter, how would that change our day? Would that change our lives? Could that change the world in which we live? Let's give ourselves the chance to find out.[1]

God did not create us to work alone in life. At the outset of our creation, God said, "It is not good for man to be alone (Genesis 2:18)." Therefore, God created family and community to let us know that we were not made to travel life alone, watch alone, wait alone, weep alone, and build alone. To transform our world, it is by divine design that humans do it together. This is why God said, "Let us make humanity in our image . . . that they take charge over all the earth (Genesis 1:26)." Notice it says, "They take charge." It was not designed at the outset of human creation that one human takes

---

1. Shawn McAndrew, "We Need Each Other," Hoffmaninstitute.org, 03/28/22.

charge but all humans who enter this world work together to take charge over the earth. The world is too big, and the responsibility of managing the earth is too large for one human, one race, and one nation to do what needs to be done to take care of the earth.

Therefore, we were made to need each other to run and transform the world that we have allowed over time to become disjointed and disfigured. Rich or poor, black or white, educated or uneducated, living uptown or downtown, we need each other to create a better world. It doesn't matter how high our IQ is; it doesn't matter how successful we are; it doesn't matter how prosperous we are; it doesn't matter how much money we have or what our social class is; we need each other to save humanity from the vices that threaten to wipe us out. We cannot do this alone; nuclear weapons have now put us in a position where we either choose non-violence or become nonexistent. We either work together to build a better world or work against each other and perish. Our existence and future are held in the balance of our choosing. We must choose to bring back national collectivism to help form a more perfect union. The progress we have made on many fronts has been done by Americans who did not let personal and political vendettas get in the way of the good of the nation. We must continue to choose to put the good of the nation before profit and politics.

We are not where we are today on our own. Somebody had to help us. Somebody had to extend a helping hand. Somebody gave us a chance. Somebody believed in us, and somebody sacrificed for us. In this mean, evil, and spiritually toxic world, we need each other to achieve visions and set goals. Wherever we are trying to go in life, however far we must travel, whatever we need to get there, somewhere on life's journey, we have to depend on others to help us get there. There is a Zambian proverb that says, "When you run alone, you run fast. But, when you run together, you run far." The life we have been called to is not a 100-yard dash! It is a marathon. We need each other on life's journey. There is no such thing as self-sufficiency. Show me someone self-sufficient who has never needed a helping hand, never needed assistance, never needed encouragement, never needed advice, comfort, and direction in life, and I will show you someone dead. In life, there is no way we can make it on our own. Life is designed so that we need others.

Any sports team demonstrates that no single player plays the game by him or herself. Every player needs other players on the team to win. It doesn't matter how much more gifted and famous one player is than other players; no player can win the game by himself or herself. Every player must play his part to win the game. They are a team. A team means more than one. Players play as a team, win as a team, and lose as a team. The team needs each other in times of victory and in times of defeat. So it is on the journey of life. Martin Luther King, Jr. helps us to understand how we are beholden to one another before we leave home.

> We do not finish breakfast without being dependent on more than half the world. When we arise in the morning, we go into the bathroom where we reach for a sponge that is provided for us by a Pacific Islander. We reach for soap that is created for us by a Frenchman. A Turk provides the towel. Then, at the table, we drink coffee, which is provided for us by a South American, tea by a Chinese, or cocoa by a West African. Before we leave [our homes], we are beholden to more than half the world. In a real sense, all life is interrelated. All men are caught in an inescapable network of mutuality, tied in a single garment of destiny. What affects one directly affects us all indirectly . . . This is the interrelated structure of reality."[2]

However, there is a future danger. The more we progress in the world of science and technology, the more we need each other because of the threat of artificial intelligence that must be monitored and held at bay. We must never allow machines to take the place of humans. Machines are impersonal and non-empathic. They cannot give the emotional and supportive human interaction we need from other human beings. It must never be forgotten that machines are tools to aid us, but they must never replace where humans should be. If we don't watch it, our interdependence on one another could be dangerously undermined by AI machines producing unintended consequences that will push us further apart than we already are.

Americans and other nations must realize how much we need each other. The world won't get any better holding on to our narrow idiosyncrasies without realizing our commonality. We don't expect musical instruments to

---

2. Martin Luther King, Jr. , *Strength to Love* (Philadelphia: Fortress Press, 1963), 70.

sound alike to have beautiful music any more than we should expect nations to be alike to have commonality. An orchestra means each player plays notes from their particular instrument. To have beautiful music across the human spectrum to achieve freedom, justice, and equality, each nation must take notes from its particular cultural perspective. It is foolish to punish one nation because its sense of freedom looks and sounds different from our own. We must learn to appreciate, not denigrate, differences in the global world. Diversity must be celebrated, not just tolerated, and this is why we say America is a nation of exceptionalism. At least, this is what it claims. Americans must first take ownership of its creed; then, it can reverberate around the world. Values that are always communicated but never activated to the full are nothing short of delusion. The world is not interested in theological, philosophical, social, and civil concepts but in the carrying out of what we say. If we cannot be true to our word, the nation cannot survive much longer on falsehoods. As much as America talks about justice and equality for all, the reality is far from the talk. If only America could be true to what she says on paper, she could close the enormous gap of inconsistency. The gap will take the willingness of us all to close.

America is still what Maya Angelo called "Yet to be the United States." There are still inconsistencies in what is proclaimed and what is practiced for all citizens. We find schism within the institution that is supposed to help provide moral and spiritual guidance for a complicated nation. We cannot help but pause and consider the wise and truthful words of H. Richard Niebuhr. "Denominationalism thus represents the moral failure of Christianity. And unless the ethics of brotherhood can gain victory over this divisiveness within the body of Christ, it is useless to expect it to be victorious in the world. But before the church can hope to overcome its fatal division, it must learn to recognize and to acknowledge the secular character of its denominationalism."[3] The postmodern church cannot expect unity within the nation when there is no unity within the church. Henry Nelson Wieman believes we have schism within the church because there lacks the power of a mature religion. He believed a mature church should work with other social institutions to achieve the common good

---

3. H. Richard Niebuhr, *The Social Sources of Denominationalism* (New York: The World Publishing Co., Meridian Books, 1957; originally 1929), 25.

for all in society. Of course, this means committed cooperation among the church and other social institutions.

> The power of a mature religion is not the ability of the church to induce or require actions of the people. Neither is it the ability of the clergy to move the people to action . . . The church and the clergy might well cooperate to induce action of all the people but only in conjunction with the other major institutions, and the concerted action would be directed primarily not to the service of the church nor the practice of any kind of religious ceremony. It would be directed to constructive action in government, industry, school, family, science, art, the professions, and in all the secular pursuits of life. The part of the church and its officials would be to deepen personal and group commitment to the common good, which is served in all these different ways. The power of action resulting from this commitment would be the power of a mature religion pervading society and the lives of the people in all they do. It would not be centered in the church any more than in family, school, government, business, and other areas of constructive action.[4]

Centuries ago, during the early church, Paul heard how the Corinthian Church was coming apart because they were using their gifts to compete rather than cooperate. He conveyed to them there is no spiritual gift greater than the other. To help the Corinthian church to have a mature religion and a coalition of cooperation, Paul used the human body to show unity. Each member of the body has a different function, but it is still part of the one body. The whole body cannot be one member for how would the rest of the body function? Paul says, "Now if the foot should say, 'Because I am not a hand, I do not belong to the body,' it would not for that reason stop being part of the body. And if the ear should say, 'Because I am not an eye, I do not belong to the body,' it would not, for that reason, stop being a part of the body. If the whole body were an eye, where would the sense of hearing be? If the whole body were an ear, where would the sense of smell be? But God has placed the parts in the body, every one of them, just as

---

4. Henry Nelson Wieman, *Creative Freedom Vocation of Liberal Religion* (New York: The Pilgrim Press, 1982), 89.

He wanted them to be. If they were all one part, where would the body be? As it is, there are many parts, but one body. The eye cannot say to the hand, I don't need you!' And the head cannot say to the feet, I don't need you (1 Corinthians 12:15-17)." Our bodies would be in bad shape if each part worked against other parts. What if our feet decided to stop functioning because they could not be on top of the shoulders? What if our knees started fussing with our arms because they disagreed about who was more important? What if our ears became angry and jealous of our eyes because they have not had a chance to be in front of the face? What if our kidneys were fighting to be where the heart is located, or our heart became angry because it is not located in the head? We would be some awful, grotesque-looking beings. But, our Creator set in place each member of our body parts so we can carry out the plans and purposes for why we exist.

As Americans and members of the human family, we need each other to transform chaos into order and gain peace from war. Until we realize our need for each other, the world will continue its downward trajectory toward destruction. The human outlook is not without hope. Social, economic, and political transformation can be imagined and rendered possible if we lay aside polarization and work with cooperation to solve the nagging problems before us. The Apostle Paul made us aware centuries ago, "For our struggle is not against flesh and blood, but against the authorities, against the powers of this dark world and the spiritual forces of evil in the heavenly realms (Ephesians 6:12)." If we want a future radically different from the present, we must turn toward God and one another to have such a future. The work of justice, equality, democracy, and spiritual warfare is not over. This struggle is ongoing. We must never accept wrong, evil, and injustice to sit on the throne and submit to it. To do so, we are less than what God is calling us to be. Together, we can be an embodiment of resistance to the unjust and inhumane powers of the world. The world does not have to be the way it is if we, the people, decide to come together and shape it another way. In a speech, Robert F. Kennedy said, "George Bernard Shaw once wrote, 'Some people see things as they are and say why? I dream things that never were and say, why not."[5] If enough people of goodwill could ask, why not a better world? Why not shape the world

---

5. Robert F. Kennedy, Remarks at the University of Kansas, March 18, 1968, jjklibrary.org

to be more just and humane? Together, we can make it happen. But, if we acquiesce to a world that is and does not dream of a world that could be, our future won't look better than our present. All that is needed to change the trajectory of our nation and the world is our awareness and cooperation that we need each other.

For many years, our nation could only see at night by oil lamps. This light was limited until two investors who were born from different racial and educational backgrounds decided to come together and improve upon giving greater light to the nation and the world. These two men were Thomas Edison and Lewis Latimer. Thomas Edison discovered the light bulb but had problems keeping the bulb lit. He tried over and over again but to no avail. The most he could do was keep the bulb lit for one to two hours at the most. People told Edison about a black man named Lewis Latimer, who discovered the filament. Latimer devised a way to help light stay lit for several hours. Edison needed Latimer's filament, and Latimer needed Edison's bulb. Because they needed each other and came together, they lit up the whole world. We have great illumination around the world because these two people understood they needed each other and made our world better. Think about what we can accomplish when we realize we need each other!

Many years ago I heard a story of a group of people traveling on the highway. They had traveled a long distance when the bus stopped at a very small town. The people got off the bus, desperately looking for the restroom. There was only one restroom, and it cost a dime to use it. The people searched for dimes, but no one had one. They searched, and they searched, but no one had a dime. An old woman with the people said, "I found a dime deep down in my bag." The people said, "We are still in desperate need because you only have one dime and how will the rest of us use the restroom?" The old woman said, "If we work together, we can get through this! When I finish in the restroom, I will hold the door open for the next person, and the next person can hold the door open for the next person until all of us have had our turn." The people solved a problem by holding the door open for one another. If we hold the door of justice, democracy, equality, goodwill, love, mercy, compassion, peace, and forgiveness open, we can create a freer and more humane world.

Chapter Two

OUR SOCIAL RESPONSIBILITY

This is what the Lord Almighty said: 'Administer true justice; show mercy and compassion to one another. Do not oppress the widow or the fatherless, the foreigner or the poor. Do not plot evil against each other.' —ZECHARIAH 7:9-10

To have a society where we can live together not only as decent people but also have a successful, peaceful country, we must have a sense of morality; we must have just laws and equal treatment under those laws; we must have good government, fair wages, access to good education, good healthcare; hold one another accountable and practice social responsibility of all members of society, regardless of race, gender, religion, class and color. When responsibility breaks down in any one of these areas, it affects the whole society. It's going to take all of us to work toward a free and just society and create the kind of nation where all people are treated with dignity and respect, and no one is left languishing on the margin of society. The power of togetherness is the creative way to create this ideal society. The more we don't cooperate, the more we lose our strength and the more we increase the power of those who rule and oppress us. A magic wand won't create this free and just society. It won't automatically blow in by the strong winds of inevitability.

We must be intentional about social responsibility, and this requires action on our part. When we fail to speak up when injustice and brutality are being inflicted upon people, what will happen when these same social injustices happen to us? It may be other people today, but what happens when we are the victims tomorrow? While we remain reticent amid people being hurt, mistreated, and run over by the forces of injustice and oppression, Martin Niemöller gives us something to ponder:

> First, they came for the Socialists, and I did not speak out,
> Because I was not a Socialist.
>
> Then they came for the Trade Unionists, and I did not speak out,
> Because I was not a Trade Unionist.
>
> Then they came for the Jews, and I did not speak out,
> Because I was not a Jew.
>
> Then they came for me,
> and there was no one left to speak for me.[1]

Christians in America cannot stand on the sidelines while social and economic injustice is flooding the streets of our cities, especially in disadvantaged areas. Our vertical relationship with God requires a horizontal relationship with others. We are our brothers and sisters' keepers. John reminds us of the importance of the vertical and horizontal relationship. "If someone says, 'I love God and hates his brother, he is a liar; for he who does not love his brother whom he has seen, how can he love God whom he has not seen (1 John 4:20.)?" Love in action is what social responsibility looks like in public. It is glimpses of the Kingdom of God in operation among humankind. Jen Arnold made this cogent observation concerning the vertical and horizontal relationship between God and humanity.

> Not by coincidence, the cross is made up of two beams of wood—one vertical and one horizontal. The vertical beam symbolizes your relationship with God, while the horizontal beam represents your relationship with others. You need both to form a cross. You need both to be a Christian . . .

1. Martin Niemoller, "First they came for the Socialists," United States Holocaust Memorial Museum in Washington, D.C. February 5, 2011.

We use the vertical to represent our relationship with God because we are inferior, and He is all-supreme . . . This vertical relationship is not passive. Imagine an electrical circuit running up and down the beam or sound waves pulsating back and forth across it. This is an active relationship with energy going up and down the beam. God extends all sorts of gifts to us, and we receive them. We offer everything back up to God, and in return, He responds . . . The horizontal beam represents our relationship with others. We know we make up the Body of Christ, and we are all connected on this horizontal plane. Everything we do affects the rest of the parcels on that beam. When we sin, it affects our neighbor. When we are charitable and loving, it also affects our neighbors. Again, this relationship between persons is not passive. Christians are called to action.[2]

The cross analogy says we cannot be only vertical Christians without being horizontal Christians at the same time. To love God is also to love mankind, and both are active. Charles C. Ryrie said, "If social responsibility is a part of the gospel it must have top priority. If it is not, then the believer must think carefully about his priorities and arrange the various opportunities of his life in biblical order. What priority should be given to social responsibilities in comparison, say, to church responsibilities, family responsibilities, or the cultivation of personal holiness? . . . We must examine what God's Word says about this area of social responsibility."[3] Although we may not know which area to give priority, one thing is clear, we cannot ignore one social responsibility for another because they are all connected. If we ignore family responsibilities this impacts society; if we ignore personal holiness, this impacts society as well. It is all interrelated and interconnected. Followers of Jesus Christ must be involved participants to bring about a just and humane society. Jesus was involved in the life of people. He served people who were in need. He did not ignore people who were pushed to the margins of society. We cannot ignore our social responsibility towards others because when we do, it affects our vertical relationship with God. If we don't get our vertical relationship with God back in alignment with God, we could forfeit our souls away from God.

---

2. Jen Arnold, "The Vertical and Horizontal Beams" Corpus Christi Catholic Church, The Body of Christ Becoming Disciples, 3/28/2020, corpuschristiphx.org

3. Charles C. Ryrie, *What You Should Know About Social Responsibility* (Chicago: Moody Press, 1982), 10.

We can't just talk about the wrong in society; we must correct the wrong; we can't just talk about politicians; we must vote them in or vote them out. We can't just talk about injustice; we must challenge it to correct it. We can't just talk about police brutality; we must challenge the police unions. The point is—to have a free and just society, requires human involvement. We are a codetermining power by our creation. We have a say so in determining what kind of society, nation, and world we want to live in. We have the power to say no to racism, sexism, terrorism, communism, and quietism. Martin Buber, the great Jewish theologian, said, "Man can choose God, and he can reject God . . . Man has the power to lead the world to perdition implies that he has the power to lead the world to redemption . . . These two powers of man constitute the actual admission of man into mightiness . . . The fact remains that the creation of this being, man, means that God has made room for a codetermining power, for a starting point for events . . ."[4] God wills to have us join Him in creating a just society.

Therefore, we must do more than pray; we must act and act collectively to usher in the kind of society we desire to live in. Like a giant puzzle with many pieces of color, each of us must bring our piece of the puzzle to have a just society. Unless you bring your piece and I bring my piece, we cannot achieve a free and just society. You might ask, "What is a free and just society? What is free and just for one group may be enslaving and unjust for another group. To answer this question, I could give you a philosophical and sociological perspective, but this would be subjective. Let me give an objective answer. The prophet Zechariah stated, "Thus says the Lord of hosts: 'Execute true justice, show mercy and compassion, everyone to his brother. Do not oppress the widow or the fatherless, the alien or the poor. Let none of you plan evil in his heart against his brother." This is the description of a free and just society. If we abide by this definition, think about how better our society would be. Think how much better our homes and communities would be. Think how more relevant our churches would be if we could live out what is described in Zechariah. This description was not given to part of society but all of society; it wasn't given to one race of

---

4. Martin Buber, cited in William R. Jones, *Is God A White Racist?* (New York: Double Day Anchor, 1973), 187–88.

people but all races of people; it was not given to one class of people but all classes of people. To achieve this kind of society is our collective social responsibility.

America is ignoring its social responsibility. Because of race, racism, and greed, America is coming apart. Our state and national leaders cannot agree on anything. Too many of our leaders are looking out for themselves and not for society as a whole. They have lost their sense of social responsibility because a great majority of voters have lost their sense of responsibility. We cannot just look at the leaders in Washington, DC, without looking at voters who are responsible for voting these leaders in office. Until we correct the lack of social responsibility among citizens, many of our leaders will continue to lead by consensus, not by conscience, endangering the foundation and moral principles that keep a civilized society stable. Ignoring social responsibility is putting at risk the people and institutions we want to protect. Insulating ourselves from others who lack basic needs in society creates a nothing-to-lose clan of people who won't care about their lives or the lives of others. In America, we are at a point of social breakdown because we have not responded in any significant way to the needs of the "least of these" in society. Until we realize our common humanity, as Eugene Debs stated, "While there is a lower class, I am in it. While there is a criminal element, I am of it. While there is a soul in prison, I am not free,"[5] we cannot maintain a stable society. A stable society cannot last long when the pillars that uphold that society are neglected and allowed to rot. When the pillars fall, the whole nation suffers regardless of social class and zip code.

The question is, how do we navigate ourselves out of this conundrum? We must first get back to the core values of our nation! There are three major core values we must go back to that will impact the rest. The first major value on which America was founded is an understanding and respect for God. The second is self-government or democracy, and the third is liberty and justice for all. In terms of God, many of the founding fathers did have a belief in God, which they called Creator. From this belief, it was reflected in America's Declaration of Independence. "We hold these truths to be self-evident, that all men are created equal, that they are endowed by their Creator with certain unalienable Rights, that among these are Life, Liberty

---

5. Eugene Debs, "Statement to the Court," *Court Stenographer*, September 18, 1918.

and the pursuit of Happiness."[6] The founding fathers desired a nation that would respect the life and liberty of all citizens because they are endowed by their Creator. When we don't respect the life and liberty of each other, we deny the Creator and a core value we should never ignore to have a stable republic.

Thomas Jefferson, the 3rd President of the United States and a signer of the US Constitution, also understood the core value of recognizing and understanding God in the life of the nation. Jefferson said, "God who gave us life gave us liberty. And can the liberties of a nation be thought secure when we have removed their only firm basis, a conviction in the minds of the people that these liberties are of the Gift of God? That they are not to be violated but with His wrath? Indeed, I tremble for my country when I reflect that God is just; that His justice cannot sleep forever . . ."[7] When we violate the gift of liberty God has given to mankind, we invoke the wrath of God. Since liberty is a core value, Jefferson knew that slavery and oppression were the antithesis of liberty.

The second core value we need to return to is self-government or democracy. When the ultra-rich are allowed to hijack the government for their agenda, this is not what the framers of the Constitution intended. Democracy should not be for sale! Too much sweat and blood went into breaking from the British authoritarian government to become a new form of authoritarianism in America. At this present time, America is on a slippery slope towards authoritarianism. The political climate of today is failing to guard democracy. More than ever before, we need to save our democracy from those who are willing to pass by and tear down the guard rails to have their way. Judge Michael Luttig stated, "Democracy is worth defending because it is the greatest method of self-governance . . . it's almost an understatement to call it genius, but the genius of democracy is that all power—all of it—comes from we the people . . . We must now come to the aid of our struggling America . . . The fact that politicians have failed us is a failure not of democracy, but failure of our elected officials to put the interests of the United States ahead of their partisan interests."[8]

6. Preamble to the Declaration of Independence, "America's Founding Documents," archives.gov
7. Notes on the State of Virginia, Query XVII, p.237.
8. Michael Luttig, "Democracy Is Worth Defending," *The Columns* by Sara Butler, columns.wlu.edu, June 2, 2023.

The third core value we must return to is liberty and justice for all. When our soldiers go off to fight, they are fighting and dying to ensure freedom and justice for all citizens of the United States. America cannot remain a thriving democratic republic when liberty and justice have not been practiced towards blacks and other citizens of color as they have with their white counterparts. A civil war was fought to guarantee this right under the 14th and 15th Amendments to the Constitution. President Lincoln stated, "We cannot survive half slave and half free."[9] The full impact of justice and equality is still lacking when it comes to people of color in the United States. The tension between what is stated in the Amendment to the Constitution and the actual practice of these guarantees is still an ongoing struggle. It is the government's responsibility to promote and protect the rights of all citizens as a core value of being an American.

But, when the government refuses to pass legislation like the John Lewis Voting Rights Bill and the George Floyd Justice Bill, tension among citizens continues to boil weakening democracy in America. Benjamin Mays believed that "Government is responsible for seeing to it that the proper environment is created where these human rights can be pursued objectively and creatively. Further, in guaranteeing human rights to all citizens, just and fair laws must be enacted, enforced, and incorporated into the political life of the nation."[10] Mays went on to say if a person has to be of a certain race or class to be treated with dignity and respect, "Then democracy is conditional rather than universal. Those ideals in the Constitution must be implemented so that democracy can function throughout the nation without regard to nationality, race, class, or caste, guaranteeing the whole citizenry free access to the economic, political, educational, and social opportunities in the system."[11]

America could be a better nation if she would treat every citizen with the same core values of rights, respect, and justice. To this day, the words we say while saluting the American flag are hollow. Our creeds and deeds don't match. Once again, Benjamin Mays gives us reason to pause:

9. Abraham Lincoln, "House Divided Speech," Springfield, Illinois, June 16, 1858, Neely, Mark E. Jr. 1982. *The Abraham Lincoln Encyclopedia* (New York, Da Capo Press), In.

10. Benjamin E. Mays, *Walking Integrity Benjamin Mays, Mentor to Martin Luther King, Jr.,* edited by Lawrence Edward Carter Sr. (Macon, GA: Mercer University Press, 1998), 271.

11. Ibid., 282.

We are what we do and not what we say. We are as democratic as we live, and we are as Christian as we act. If we talk about brotherhood and segregate human beings, we do not believe in brotherhood. If we talk about democracy and deny it to certain groups, we do not believe in democracy. If we preach justice and exploit the weak, we do not believe in justice. If we preach truth and tell lies, we do not believe in truth. We are what we do.[12]

It is very difficult for black people to believe in American justice because, for too long, they have been the victims of injustice. Only God keeps black people believing in a nation that constantly shortchanges them with justice. What does justice look like in life? Howard Thurman stated, "Social justice is defined as a condition in which every person has and does peacefully what it is his right to have and to do; he fills the place for which he is fitted . . . Once it is assumed that men are born with the basic equipment that defines their place and function in society, then each is fulfilled when this potential is realized. From this point of view, even the notion of justice is derived."[13]

America has a long way to go in practicing its democratic creed. If America wants the rest of the world to believe in its democratic philosophy, then America must demonstrate justice to all of its citizens at home. America cannot criticize other nations for human rights violations when justice is violated in its homeland. Justice is not a white race, black race, or any race invention. "Justice belongs to God and doesn't belong to man. And any man who tries to administer justice to his fellow man based on superiority and inferiority is taking unto himself the role of God."[14] The challenge to America is to live up to its democratic creed regardless of race, religion, nationality, and class or be a nation of liars.

---

12. Ibid., 254.
13. Howard Thurman, *The Search For Common Ground, An Inquiry Into The Basis Of Man's Experience Of Community* (Richmond, IN: Friends United Press, 1971), 48–49.
14. Benjamin Mays, *Walking Integrity*, 267–68.

Chapter Three

WE NEED CONSTRUCTIVE DISRUPTION

There's nothing more fundamentally disruptive to the status quo than a new reality. —UMAIR HAQUE

It is a historical fact that most—if not all—of the social changes that have happened in our world involve some form of disruption. The freedoms we enjoy in America came through some form of disruption. From the Boston Tea Party to the abolitionist movement to the civil rights struggle to the women's liberation movement—all involved disruption. For us to experience transformation in our nation, we must engage in some form of constructive disruption. Unless we disrupt the present cultural, social, economic, and political order of our day, transformation won't come. Afeni Shakur said, "Trust me, you can't change anything without causing some degree of disruption. It's impossible; that is exactly what change is. Some people are uncomfortable with the disruption that change causes, but the disruption is necessary if anything is going to change."[1] Robert Scobie stated, "Change is inevitable, and the disruption that it causes often brings both inconvenience and opportunity."[2]

People may be uncomfortable with the word disruption, but we are all engaged in it in some form or another. For example, when we get sick and

1. Shalom, Kate, Kateshopecafe.net, November 11, 2022.
2. Ibid.

go to the doctor, that disrupts the sickness that could kill us. When we call the exterminator, he comes to disrupt the infestation of insects. Exercising is an act of disruption to bad health. Cease eating certain foods that are not good for us is an act of disruption. Obeying God is disrupting curses and bad consequences. Getting an education is disrupting ignorance; going to work is disrupting having no income. Saving and investing money is disrupting poverty. Watering plants disrupts the dryness that could kill the plants. Getting married disrupts ungodliness. Loving ourselves disrupts self/hatred. Correcting children is disrupting their path to destruction. Praying to God through Christ is disrupting the power of the enemy over us. When we vote, we are disrupting antidemocratic forces. Whatever we do to prevent wrong, evil, injustice, sickness, disease, and death is a form of disruption. The point is we participate in disruptions all the time without realizing we are doing it. The same is needed to transform our nation and the world.

There is no question our nation has lost most of its moral and spiritual values and we see the manifestation of this playing out every day somewhere in America. There is so much evil, injustice, and corruption in our nation that people are wondering if we are on demonic steroids. We are reaching new lows of wickedness, and it is disturbing to witness the moral and spiritual collapse of our nation, which is supposed to be Christian. If there isn't a moral and spiritual disruption to transform our nation, life gets worse for all of us! We are at a point in which we either disrupt the dangerous decadence going on in our nation or stand back and allow the dissipation of our democratic foundation to continue. The foundation of America has had deep cracks in it for a long time, but too many Americans of goodwill are sitting back while the nation is about to topple and fall. Too many Christians are on the sidelines while the Kingdom of God is calling them to get involved in the transformation of their local churches, schools, communities, and nation.

While the culture of racial hatred and violence is rapidly increasing, too many Americans are turning their heads and hearts away. While children and young people are being ravaged by death-producing conditions that bring about their early demise, too many Americans have become desensitized. Too many of our political leaders are caught up in politicizing issues that need bipartisan solutions. Mass shootings have become commonplace to the point we don't know how to navigate ourselves out of this conundrum without lawsuits being filed against Second Amendment rights. America has become a childish nation, and we wonder why our respectability around the world is waning. Fear, division, wickedness, misinformation, violence, and political bickering over nonsense have made our nation less safe and less productive. America needs to stop the nonsense and start using common sense so life can make sense.

The only thing that can arrest and transform our cultural, social, economic, and political situation is collective moral and spiritual disruption. This disruption is not about violence, rioting, and being destructive. We have too much of this already in a world of pain and division. What is needed is a constructive disruption, which means noncooperation with wrong, evil, and injustice. When we don't cooperate with what divides us and causes human suffering, we take away the steam that gives power to the engine of oppression. To bring down the high cost of food, gas, and water takes noncooperation. When we find a way to reduce the demand for necessities by not cooperating with greed—that will force companies to bring prices down to affordable levels. We should never doubt the power of collective noncooperation with evil. Mahatma Gandhi, who was jailed many times for his human rights struggle, stated at one trial, "In my humble opinion, non-cooperation with evil is as much a duty as is cooperation with good."[3] Noncooperation with the unjust status quo can create positive tension in the nation that would encourage us to come and reason together to change the destructive trajectory of the nation. American democracy is in the critical care unit, hooked up to a life support system of which it could die at any time. Unless we rise and disrupt antidemocratic forces in America, don't be surprised if we wake up one morning living in a totalitarian republic. Don't be surprised what we fought against abroad is not won at home. If we are afraid to engage in moral and spiritual disruption, there is no need to continue to sing our national anthem.

The question is what kind of nation do we want for ourselves and our children and future generations? Are we willing to sacrifice to pass on a

---

3. Mahatma Gandhi, "Gandhi and Civil Disobedience" Teach Democracy formerly Constitutional Rights Foundation, 2023, crf-usa.org

better nation to the next generation? Are we brave enough to engage in disruption to create a better nation? Are we conscience enough to speak truth to power? Are we willing to move from thermometers to thermostats to set the nation back on a path of becoming a more perfect union? If the United States Constitution with its amendments is being discarded and trampled upon, and we don't have enough citizens who have a love of country to stop the practice of desecration of our governing documents, then the nation can no longer be called "American exceptionalism." Abraham Lincoln reminds us, "Don't interfere with anything in the Constitution. That must be maintained, for it is the only safeguard of our liberties. And not to Democrats alone do I make this appeal, but to all who love these great and true principles."[4]

Not struggling and defending what America stands for at home makes us a joke abroad. The old saying goes, "Charity begins at home and then spreads abroad." If, at home, we refuse to engage in moral and spiritual disruption for justice, equality, humanity, and the preservation of the U.S. Constitution, how authentic are we when we encourage it abroad? The point is if we truly believe in democracy, equality, and fairness, let us first demand and practice it at home so we may be an example aboard. When the nations of the world see our disruptions against people, practices, and policies that threaten the US Constitution and its amendments, it is more believable abroad. To continue to be a leader of the free world, we must first lead at home. Let us be the practitioners of our governing documents before we go and speak of them abroad.

No nation has ever become more just and humane without disruptions. Ancient history reveals that God sent Moses to liberate His people from the bondage of Egypt, and Pharaoh refused, therefore God disrupted Egypt's social order. God disrupted their weather; their economy, and the whole status quo of Egypt. When God is dissatisfied with His people, He sends prophets to disrupt their ways with the hope they repent or regret. The Tower of Babel is another example of disruption in which God caused people to speak different languages so they could not understand one another in the effort to build a skyscraper to reach heaven. Just think what would have happened to the Jewish people had not Queen Esther

4. Abraham Lincoln, Speech at Kalamazoo, Michigan, August 27, 1856, Abraham lincoln.org

disrupted a genocide plan by exposing the person behind the plot. God always uses people who are called to engage in disruptions to bring about significant change.

The life of Jesus Christ is the greatest disruption in the world. He entered this world to disrupt Satan's hostile kingdom of darkness by preaching the Kingdom of God and demonstrating its power over darkness. The disruption of God through Jesus Christ provides salvation to those enslaved by sin and oppression. Jesus tells us He didn't come to this world to go along to get along. He said, "Do not think that I came to bring peace on earth. I did not come to bring peace but a sword. For, I have come to 'set a man against his father, a daughter against her mother, and a daughter-in-law against her mother-in-law'; and a man's enemies will be those of his household. He who loves father or mother more than Me is not worthy of Me. And he who loves son or daughter more than Me is not worthy of Me. And he who does not take his cross and follow after Me is not worthy of Me. He who finds his life will lose it, and he who loses his life for My sake will find it (Matthew 10:34-39.)"

Jesus came to disrupt the order of this ungodly world. He didn't come to placate us! He didn't come to get caught up in our false peace. He didn't come to participate in non-liberating activities and political divisions. Jesus came to be a disruption to the works of Satan and to give His life as a ransom for many. He came to disrupt sin and its consequences. To be His disciple, we, too, must engage in constructive disruption. The movement Jesus started not only disrupted the religious and political life of the Roman Empire, but He established the church to continue the disruption against sin, evil, and injustice! Therefore, the church was established to be a disruption for the Kingdom of God in this world. However, over time, the church lost its way. Instead of the church being a disruption against evil, injustice, and oppression, the church became the endorser and the guarantor of this dark and evil world. To get back to the purpose for which it was established, the church must repent and become the disruption it is supposed to be.

The church has missed too many opportunities to impact the world for the Kingdom of God. Had enough people of goodwill in the church of Germany engaged in moral and spiritual disruption, it would have saved millions of souls killed by Hitler's regime. In the early formulation of

America, had enough professing Christians aggressively engaged in disruption, slavery and oppression could have been prevented. As a nation, we wouldn't be plagued by racism and its manifestations today had the church been a disruption yesterday. We may be uncomfortable with the term disruption, but understand, no disruption, no democracy; no disruption, no progress; no disruption, no advancements; no disruption, no transformation! America cannot sustain the way things are going for much longer. The urgency of the time is for the church and American people to engage again in moral and spiritual disruption, especially in this American empire.

This also means we must tell the truth and expose the lies. There is too much intentional misinformation on the airways and in the headlines. Lies cause us to mistrust one another, and this mistrust further divides the nation. If we cannot trust our leaders and institutions, we are on the verge of a national breakdown. Gerald Baker, the editor at large for *The Wall Street Journal*, stated:

> Civic institutions in which Americans once placed their confidence have also seen drastic declines in trust. Trust in churches has been undermined by declining religious observance and shocking clerical scandals; labor unions, in retreat in the private sector but ever dominant in the public sector, are increasingly seen as pursuing self-serving and politically motivated ends; even voluntary institutions such as community groups, social clubs, and charitable organizations have been abandoned in a country that has become more atomized and its citizens more isolated from one another.
>
> Above all, this broad loss of trust in institutions contributed to sharply declining levels of trust among Americans themselves. The basic faith people have in other citizens to play by the rules, obey the law, and accept their wider social responsibilities is as essential to a nation's success as the human capital of its population and the economic capital of business. But in the last ten years, survey data indicates that millions of Americans have stopped trusting one another. This pathology of distrust across American society is eating the country away from the inside.[5]

5. Gerard Baker, *American Breakdown Why We No Longer Trust Our Leaders and Institutions and How We Can Rebuild Confidence* (New York: Hachette Book Group, 2023), 14.

Moreover, James Comey, the former FBI Director, stated, "Dangerous time when our country is led by those who will lie about anything, backed by those who will believe anything, based on information from media sources that will say anything. Americans must break out of that bubble and seek truth."[6] Unless this happens, the words of Abraham Lincoln will move from possibility to factuality. "If destruction is our lot, we must ourselves be its author and finisher. As a nation of freemen, we must live through all time or die by suicide."[7] We must disrupt wrong, evil, and injustice! We must disrupt systematic racism, discrimination, and exploitation. To be the salt of the earth and light of the world, the postmodern church needs to get out of bed with the world and do God's Will on earth as it is in heaven.

We don't have to accept the nation and the world as they are; we have disruption power to make the world what it can be! Honest dissent doesn't mean hatred of the country; it means sounding the alarm signal of a country that is on the road to destruction. We are at a point where we either stand up and disrupt the dangerous decadence of our nation or stand down and allow the dissipation of our democratic foundation to crumble until it is irreparable. The only thing that can arrest and transform our unjust world is moral and spiritual disruption. Together, we have enough disruption power to encourage America to chart a different course. We have enough disruption power to not only tear down what destroys us but also to build up what promotes the general welfare of the people of America and around the world.

I have noticed over the years how the car industry recalls cars that have defective parts that could cause injury or death. To avoid being sued, the industry recalls cars and notifies customers of the recall. This recall says they are aware of a problem and are willing to fix it before tragedy strikes. Since this is true for the car industry, why can't we employ this same strategy and recall a broken system based on racism, oppression, and white supremacy? This unjust system has tragically destroyed lives and is still causing nightmares for many. When will America commit to recalling this broken system, fixing it, and making restitution to the injured and

---

6. James Comey, *Politico.com,* by Cristiano Lima, May, 23, 2018.

7. Abraham Lincoln, Address Before the Young Men's Lyceum of Springfield, January 27, 1838, Abraham lincoln.org.

descendants who the system has destroyed on a multiplicity of levels? If the car industry, the food industry, and others can do this to right a wrong, why can't the nation do this in terms of the American system? Many, especially white people, say they didn't create the system and, thereby, should not be blamed for how it negatively impacts people of color. We understand that many whites who make this claim are correct, but this doesn't negate the fact that the system is broken, its foundation is still racist and that whites still benefit from it today. What must be understood is although we didn't construct the system, it is our responsibility to correct it. As America was forced to correct and tear down institutional slavery, Jim and Jane Crow, it is our Christian and American duty to correct what divides, separates, and pushes us apart. Tony Evans reminds us:

> While an individual today may not be personally racist, they can contribute to the racist structures by supporting the inequitable systems still in place or by denying that they exist. If you are non-racist yourself but do not actively oppose racism (willing to speak or work against racism and racist systems where they show up), you are failing to fulfill the whole letter of the law of love (Rom. 13:8) . . . Sin is not just a bad behavior you do but rather sin is also knowing something good to do, and choosing not to do it (James 4:17; Isa. 58) . . . I have seen a tremendous increase in virtue-signaling and social media posting about racial unity over the last few years but what I have not seen much at all is any real changes in the racial integration relationships, Christian organizations' staff or church makeup, or even personal investment in addressing the broken systems that continue to plague pockets of our land. Reading a book is great. Posting about it online gets the word out. Also, good. But when you close this book, seek to do something to make a difference for good in the world in which we live. [8]

Make no mistake about it: it is going to take all of us people of goodwill and our collective power to bring a resolution to this nagging national problem. Let us not take for granted our collective power and how we can

---

8. Tony Evans, *Kingdom Race Theology God's Answer To Our Racial Crisis* (Chicago: Moody Publishers, 2022), 36–37.

be a moral and spiritual leaven in a nation that is desperately in need of transformation. Who knows, this may be our last opportunity to engage in meaningful moral and spiritual disruption before humanity destroys itself. It may be our finest hour yet to make America a better nation. It is my hope and prayer that we understand we need each other to save our nation and the world, and it is time to demonstrate that the Kingdom of God is at hand. If not us, then who? If not now, when? If our nation is destroyed from within, we have a hand in it. If our nation is transformed, we have a hand in it. Let us make sure our hands are being used for the transformation of the nation. Constructive disruption has always been encouraged and empowered by people of faith. Social movements for transformation need "Symbols, rituals, narratives, icons, and songs. They use these to contract their collective identities, to nurture solidarity, to express their grievances, and to draw inspiration and strength in difficult times. Religion, as a major creator and custodian of powerful symbols, rituals, icons, narratives, songs, testimonies, and oratory, is well-positioned to lend these sacred, expressive practices to the cause of political activism."[9]

When the Holy Spirit fuels social, economic, and political activism, it sustains social movements for the long haul, as it did with the American abolitionist movement of the nineteenth century and the civil rights movement of the twentieth century. These movements were spiritual movements that inspired, encouraged, and empowered those struggling for freedom, justice, dignity, and humanity. We are in desperate need in this twenty-first century for a movement of spiritual constructive disruption to save the United States of America and beyond. Time is ticking out for America's salvation. Unless we allow the Holy Spirit to infuse our decisions, America is doomed.

---

9. Christian Smith, Editor, *Disruptive Religion The Force of Faith in Social Movement Activism* (New York: Routledge Press, 1996), 11.

Chapter Four

BEAR ONE ANOTHER'S BURDEN

We may not be able to alter the journey, but we can make sure no one walks it alone. —ELDER JEFFREY R. HOLLAND

To live life is to live with burdens. Burdens may differ for many people, but all humans carry burdens. The rich have the burden of keeping what they have, and the poor have the burden of not having enough. Because we live in a fallen, torn, oppressive, racist, greedy, violent, sin-filled world, burdens are inevitable. Many people are crushed by their burdens, and many others have been able to overcome their burdens with the help of others. To make our communities, society, and the world better, we must bear one another's burdens. This doesn't mean to take up someone else's responsibility but to come alongside those who are suffering and struggling with burdens to help the load be easier until ultimately we can rid the causes of these burdens. Regardless of how long it takes, we need to come alongside those who are hurting, suffering, wounded, and hopeless. People need to know they are not struggling alone in this world of injustice and that there are people who care about their situation and circumstances.

We must understand that getting involved in other people's lives to lift their burdens can be very dangerous. It could cost you your life. Great leaders and people of goodwill like Frederick Douglass, Henry Lloyd Garrison,

Harriet Tubman, Mahatma Gandhi, Martin Luther King, Jr. Viola Liuzzo, James Reeb, Fannie Lou Hamer, and many others came alongside suffering people to help them bear the load of the effects of oppression, racism, sexism, exploitation, social and educational neglect. Helping to bear the load with people shows we share in their struggles to be free from the heavy yoke that has been placed upon them. "We can illustrate the idea of bearing one another's burdens with the picture of a man staggering beneath a heavy load of grain. He must somehow get this grain home to his family, but he is about to crumble beneath its weight. A brother sees his distress and rushes to his aid, lifting a part of the burden and thereby easing the weight of it. Although the supportive one does not assume the whole load, his help allows the struggling one to carry on to his destination."[1]

Many people are carrying heavy burdens in silence, and this is the reason many of them are crushed by their heavy loads. We must pay attention to those who are suffering and enter their situation to help them avoid carrying burdens by themselves. Barbara Comito stated, "We must move into the messiness of people's lives. Turning away and claiming, "It's not my business" isn't loving. It's biblical."[2] Just think if the Samaritan in the parable of Jesus had failed to help the man who had been beaten and robbed and left for dead. The man would have likely died, but because the Samaritan decided to enter the messy situation, not knowing if it was safe or staged for him to be robbed, the Samaritan took the risk and aided the man and paid for his further aid in the inn. To better our world and bear one another's burdens, we must act in like fashion as the Samaritan and enter situations and circumstances that may not be safe nor convenient to help others bear their burdens. We need more Good Samaritans to muster up enough courage to enter suffering communities where people are trapped in economic and social conditions beyond their control. Because people are experiencing hard times; because they have been dragged through social, economic, and political mud; because the stench of injustice is upon them, and the odor of neglect has penetrated their clothes, people still have value; they still have worth; they still have significance; they still have

---

1. got questions.org "What does it mean to bear one another's burdens?" (Galatians 6:2)
2. Barbara Comito, "2020 Vision: Bear One Another's Burdens," blog.uniongospelmission.org, October 8, 2020.

endowment; they still have the image of God, and this is enough to aid them on the Jericho road of life.

Due to structural injustice, large sections of society don't see the heavy burdens of others. Highways that run through and around poor suffering communities are often overlooked, and as the saying goes, "Out of sight, out of mind." When we don't see suffering humanity, how can we help lift their burdens and repave their Jericho roads? If we are honest, subconsciously, we know disadvantaged people are bearing heavy burdens to survive; but our highways and byways keep them out of sight to help ease our conscience. However, the conscience cannot be eased for too long. Conscience is the inner voice of moral responsibility we suppress over and over again to do something about suffering people. We overlook or put out of our minds people who are in need until we are reminded of it again and again. Until we act on our moral responsibility, the voice of conscience will constantly nudge us to move toward doing something. How long this nudging takes place within us no one can tell, but until we act, I believe it is always there buried under levels of blockage to our moral and spiritual sensibilities. Conscience may not provide the information but it provides the guidance needed to steer us in the right direction towards taking action. Intuitively, we know the unjust burdens the disadvantaged have to carry are predicated upon structural injustice and oppression. The socioeconomic system is not fair, and this unfairness creates unfair burdens in several disadvantaged communities. Conscience tells us the situation is not just and for us to get involved to help lift the burdens of victims of this unfairness. We may not feel like involving ourselves but conscience somehow informs us this is the right thing to do.

Back in November 2017, Edward Feser gave a lecture on "What is Conscience and When We Follow It?" He surmised that conscience is not feeling but your intellect informing you what to do when your feelings are not in line with your conscience:

> So, conscience is not a feeling. However, feelings can affect one's conscience. When things are functioning properly, they affect it by reinforcing your inclination to do what your intellect has correctly told you that you ought to do. Consider . . . your friend's suggestion that

you steal some money from the tip jar. You tell him: "No, that would be wrong." Suppose, however, that your friend responds: "But we need money for the bus, and if we get back late, we'll miss the game." Now you are tempted. Your intellect entertains the thought of missing the big game and how unpleasant this would be. This seems to give you a reason to take the money after all. It distracts your intellect's attention away from the fact that the action would nevertheless be wrong and thus should not be done even if, in other respects, taking the money would afford you a benefit. This is where the feeling of guilt steps in. It prods the intellect to direct its attention back again to moral considerations and not be distracted by the benefit that stealing might afford you. Ideally, the feelings of guilt are strong enough that they overwhelm the feelings of pleasure you get when entertaining the thought of getting back in time to watch the big game. The feelings, in that case, facilitate your resistance to temptation. They help you finally to say: "Sure, we don't want to be late, but stealing the money would be wrong so I won't do it."[3]

If only we would follow the voice of conscience and not allow the benefits of doing wrong to distract the conscience, we could be part of the solution, not part of the problem in our nation. For example, when the voice of conscience informs a person that dumping toxic waste in and near poor communities, be it in the air or water, he should not do it. Regardless of the benefit to the company he works for, he should refuse to do it. However, if he decides to do it, he has ignored the voice of conscience to be overridden by dysfunctional feelings of guilt. "The feelings of guilt are put in us by nature to facilitate our doing what our conscience tells us we should do, just as affectionate feels are put into us by nature to facilitate our willingness of what is good for another."[4] This action not only hurts the community where the toxic waste is dumped, but it also affects more affluent communities. Since water and air travel, it is not out of the realm of possibility that the effects of toxic waste can penetrate well-insulated systems. Therefore, we do well to come together and work to eliminate the causes of suffering for others to ensure the health of us all. We need to listen to the voice of conscience if we are to improve human relations.

---

3. Edward Feser, "What is Conscience and When Should We Follow It?" A lecture given at the Holy Rosary Parish Philosophy Conference in Portland, OR on November 4, 2017.

4. Ibid.

Too often, we leave out of the equation justice when discussing race, class, religion, zip code, etc. To build a just society, we must first acknowledge the humanity of all people and that there is no supreme race of people. Regardless of race, creed, or color each of us has gifts and talents that could be used to create a just society if given a chance to do so. When we deny certain groups the opportunity to equally play their part in the creation of a just society, we deprive ourselves. Research reveals when people feel connected and have a stake in the building of a just society, they are more likely to protect rather than destroy it. The opposite happens when they don't feel connected and have no stake in society.

John Dunn reminds us, "No man is an island, entire of itself; every man is a piece of the continent, a part of the main; any man's death diminishes me, because I am involved in mankind, and therefore never send to know for whom the bell tolls; it tolls for thee."[5] In America, we all carry the burden of being "One nation, under God, indivisible with liberty and justice for all." This means we must pay attention and not ignore what is happening in our nation. If democracy means anything, it means paying attention to what is happening to the poor, the oppressed, and the marginalized. When we don't pay attention to what is happening in our social institutions, to our children, to the school, and criminal justice system, we may wake up one morning in an authoritarian totalitarian nation. Let us not forget that Democracy is an idea that can be replaced with another idea if we refuse to pay attention. We must never get distracted by outright lies and political agendas to take our eyes off justice, righteousness, equality, and democracy. What happens in America is our burden to bear. Regardless of race, religion, and political representation, the burden is on us to make America a better, safer, and more humane nation.

American liberties are not sustainable unless we collectively sustain them. American freedoms are not guaranteed unless we protect them. American democracy is not assured unless we assure it. Accountability and transparency are not self-evident unless we make them so. The burden is on our shoulders to pass on a better America to our children and their children and generations to come. This means we must start with our families, our churches, our schools, our communities, and our local, state, and national

---

5. John Dunn, allpoetry.com

government. The burden is on our collective shoulders to move America from moral shame to national respect. If we don't do it, who will? If not now, when? We cannot reimagine a better society, a better government, a better nation, better schools, and better policing without bearing the burden together.

Jesus Christ, the greatest human being that ever entered our world, needed help to bear the burden of the cross to free humanity from death, hell, and destruction. If Jesus accepted help while carrying his burden, we need to allow others to help us bear our load as well. There is no need to suffer in silence. We need each other to put an end to the burden of racial hatred, white supremacy, injustice, and inequality. These social inequalities may not affect affluent communities, but it is our responsibility to help bear the burden of correcting them. Benign neglect of inequalities only leads to an evil society that keeps affluent communities on edge by looking over their shoulders, hoping not to be victimized by those who have no stake in society and who feel the American dream has been ripped away from them. They don't have anything to lose. Frederick Douglass said, "Where justice is denied, where poverty is enforced, where ignorance prevails, and where any class is made to feel that society is an organized conspiracy to oppress, rob, and degrade them, neither persons nor property will ever be safe."[6]

To remove this uneasiness in society, especially in affluent communities, we need to come together and understand that oppression is a burden; racism is a burden, injustice is a burden; inequality is a burden; poverty is a burden; exploitation is a burden; police brutality is a burden; miseducation is a burden; lack of opportunity is a burden; telling the truth is a burden. It is a burden not just for the disadvantaged communities but it is a burden for the whole nation. Whatever happens in one community will eventually happen in other communities. Whatever hatred is heaped upon one group of people will be heaped upon other groups. Whatever violence is directed toward one group will soon make its way to other people. When toxicity enters the water stream, it soon flows out to affect others. Martin Luther King, Jr. stated, "Whatever affects one directly affects all indirectly. I can

---

6. Frederick Douglass, Speech on "Southern Barbarism" in 1886 on the 24th Anniversary of Emancipation, Washington, D. C.

never be what I ought to be until you are what you ought to be. This is the interrelated structure of reality."[7]

The reason there is a breakdown in moral values and principles, many people who have the means and the power don't want to help bear the social and economic burdens of the nation. The tax breaks for the rich create a greater burden on the nation already drowning in massive debt. The rich don't mind gaining more, but they refuse to make sacrifices financially to put the nation in a solvent situation without hurting the poor and working class. Selfishness and greed are putting our nation on the wrong trajectory. There needs to be checks and balances with capitalism. The ultra-rich must understand that workers don't mind companies and industries making profits. What is desired by the working class is a share of the profits by providing a just income, fair housing, and good basic healthcare. Workers need pay increases to keep up with the cost of living. It is an American shame for workers to produce products they cannot afford to purchase.

Workers know the value of their work; though they have the muscle, they are not without a mind to think for themselves. "When Americans insisted, with one voice, that labor was the source of all value, they were not simply repeating a theoretical truism. The labor theory of value was more than an abstract principle of political economy in a country where labor's contribution to the general well-being took the form of mind as well as muscle. American mechanics, it was said, 'are not untaught operatives, but an enlightened, reflective people, who not only know how to use their hands but are familiar with principles.'"[8] Again, the issue is not opposing the amassing of wealth but its unjust distribution to the workers who help to create the wealth. Wealth doesn't destroy a nation; its unjust distribution does. The wealthy must understand they have a responsibility to those who generate wealth for them.

The Bible says, "Command those who are rich in this present world not to be arrogant nor to put their hope in wealth, which is so uncertain, but to put their hope in God, who richly provides us with everything for our enjoyment. Command them to do good deeds and to be generous and willing to share. In this way, they will lay up treasure for themselves as a

---

7. Martin Luther King, Jr. "Letter From the Birmingham Jail," August, 1963.

8. Christopher Lasch, *The Revolt Of the Elites And The Betrayal of Democracy* (New York: W.W. Norton & Company, 1995), 60.

firm foundation for the coming age, so that they may take hold of the life that is truly life (1 Timothy 6:17-19)." The least companies and industries can do is lighten the load on their employees by giving them just wages and benefits. The working class of our nation deserves more respect and more social and economic justice. They are the GNP backbone of America. To hurt the working class is to hurt the economy and the moral fiber that holds the nation together. It is unconscionable to cut off the hand that feeds you. To say this another way, why damage the lives of the very people who are making you substantial profits year after year? If you don't care about the engine that gets you where you need to go, eventually, the engine stops, and you are now strained on the road of life. So it is with workers. If companies and industries don't take care of their workforce, they could disrupt profit-making opportunities. It is in the best interest of companies and industries to do justly towards their workforce. This would not only create loyalty to the business but also eliminate the need for strikes and bad press.

Many voices from disadvantaged communities are tired of fighting battles of racism, injustice, inequality, exploitation, and police brutality in a nation they love but a nation that won't love them in return. The load disadvantaged communities have had to carry for years has worn them down, and many of them are losing hope in America. They are tired because only a few people with the power and resources are willing to struggle alongside them for justice and equality. The goal is justice and equality. It is a tough battle to overcome when the nation refuses to help bear the burden it puts on black people who have been loyal citizens. America must understand the burden it has put on people of color for centuries of oppression cannot be lifted by a few social and political handouts. What is needed is economic justice through forms of reparations so black people can participate in economic decisions that affect them and their future. For what black people have given to this nation, reparations are the least the nation can do. America has given reparations to the Jews, Japanese, and Native Americans but has not to this day given any reparations to the very people who laid the economic foundation for the nation. Black people are still waiting for the economic and social justice they deserve after their ancestors gave blood, sweat, and tears in a land that was supposed to be the home of the brave and the land of the free.

This doesn't mean coming alongside them to assume the whole load of social and economic uplift. It means helping to lighten the load of what centuries of oppression have done to them socially, economically, and psychologically. Helping to heal injured people can help better America as a whole. Helping to feed the hungry, clothe the naked, provide shelter over people's heads, take care of the elderly, and aid others who are going through tough economic times are prime examples of a responsible nation that shares in the burden of its citizens. Better still, restructuring existing structures would allow justice, equality, and love of the country to flourish, which would have lasting effects for generations to come. Let us not think restructuring existing structures would be impossible. We restructure companies and industries all the time for greater profit and productivity. Why not do it for justice and equality? Think what could happen if the whole economic and social system is restructured to have a level playing field? Think of the loyalty this would generate for the nation. Think of how disadvantaged communities could transform their neighborhoods because they now have the resources and access to do so and the support from society. The haves who give from their abundance will still have, and the have-nots can now have something to build for themselves. Economic and social justice can go a long way in forging a better future for the nation.

When we bear one another's burdens, we create what Martin Luther King, Jr. called the beloved community of which "The end is reconciliation; the end is redemption; the end is the creation of the Beloved Community. It is this type of spirit and this type of love that can transform opponents into friends. It is this type of understanding goodwill that will transform the deep gloom of the old age into the exuberant gladness of the new age. It is this love which will bring about miracles in the hearts of men."[9] The beloved community is looking out for the "least of these" with love. "When someone staggers, we help steady the load. If he is straining, we help bear the burden. And if he stumbles, we lift him. Helping fellow believers carry the weight of their worldly troubles is one of the chief practical duties that ought to consume every Christian."[10] No longer will justice and equality be

9. Martin Luther King, Jr., "*Facing the Challenge of a New Age,*" 1956, wearethebelovedcommunity.org
10. John MacArthur, "Bearing One Another's Burdens," January 1, 2010, ligonier.org

lofty ideas of a distance utopia but a common practice in our nation that could influence the world.

Together, we can build and go higher in democracy and moral excellence; we can snatch victory out of the jaws of defeat; we can transform the old world into a new world of love, light, and liberty. We go further when we lift burdens together; we achieve more when we work together! Humanity has done it before, and we can do it again. God recognized the human potential when they came together as one. The Lord said, "If as one people speaking the same language . . . then nothing they plan to do will be impossible for them (Genesis 11:6)." Whatever humans set their hearts and minds to accomplish, they can accomplish it because of the power of unity. We can achieve our goals if we bear one another's burden in the process of creating a new world out of the old world of hate, fear, division, and disunity.

Chapter Five

DON'T SELL OUT YOUR SOUL

Selling out is usually more a matter of buying in. Sell out, and you're buying into someone else's system of values, rules, and rewards. —BILL WATTERSON

There is no question we are living in times of great sellout. People and leaders are selling out their souls, their country, and their conscience for the gain of money, power, and possessions. Many of our social institutions are selling out to the rich and powerful. Many entertainers are selling out to have fame and fortune. With all of this selling out going on, is there anything not for sale? We live in a nation where moral principles are not in the equation, where profit is a concern; where power is paramount over moral values, and capitalism is more important than citizenship. To get ahead in this world, people are lowering themselves to do anything. They forsake conscience to have commodities. They overlook fairness to have financial leverage. They sell out their people to prosper and engage in inordinate selfishness to have success. All of these pursuits are not only destroying our nation but the very foundation on which America was founded—the family.

It is abysmally sad to see people selling out their families, their children, their communities, their race, their churches, their leaders, and their country to get something from the power brokers of the world. The insatiable urge for power, status, visibility, and recognition, people forsake God and His Kingdom to have these things. It is sad to see Christians running after these things at the expense of losing their souls. Edwin Lutzer stated, "Money, which is so essential for us to live, can also be the lure that makes us willing to sell our souls."[1] It is not that we shouldn't have material possessions but how we acquire them is what matters. If we sell ourselves to acquire these things, we set up ourselves to be used by the enemy to operate against what is right, what is just, and what is acceptable to God. God never wants us to pursue what the enemy offers at the expense of casting God and His Kingdom aside to acquire them. If God and His Kingdom are easily cast aside for worldly possessions, God was never possessed by those who do it in the first place. What we don't possess in heart and mind can be easily let go. Benjamin Franklin is quoted as saying, "Any society that would give up a little liberty to gain a little security will deserve neither and lose both.'"[2] It starts slow and then becomes a full-fledged throttle of giving up oneself to gain security. Once giving up on oneself starts, it won't stop until the whole person has sold out his soul.

This is why I am not surprised when some Hollywood actors, entertainers, sports players, religious and political leaders, etc., sell their souls to the highest bidder. For fame and fortune, they give up spiritual values and eternal life for temporary gain. Jesus said, "For what will it profit a man if he gains the whole world and loses his soul? Or what will a man give in exchange for his soul (Mark 8:36-37)?" Jesus wants people to know that their souls are the most prized possessions in the world, and if people sell out their souls, they have made the worst tradeoff that a human being can make. After they have traded their souls for temporary possessions and enjoyed them for a season, their souls will be held accountable to God the very next season. "Just as people are destined to die once, and after that to face judgment (Hebrews 9:27)." It is unconscionable to give up an eternal treasure for fleeting gain. For this reason, Moses "Chose to be mistreated along with the people of God rather than enjoy the fleeting pleasures of sin (Hebrews 11:25)." Jesus emptied himself by giving up all his power, glory, majesty, and lowered himself to come to serve and save humanity from sin (Philippians 2:7). The example Jesus demonstrated

---

1. Erwin W. Lutzer, *When A Nation Forgets God, 7 Lessons We Must Learn From Nazi Germany* (Chicago: Moody Publishers, 2010), 47.

2. Ibid, 48.

to us is when we desire to go up, we must go down. Most people follow the devil's example of going up and ending down. Until we are willing to empty ourselves of pride, supremacy, arrogance, and greed by coming down to serve suffering humanity as Moses, Jesus, and many others have done for their transformation, we can be assured we will never go up to be a part of the glory to come.

Pleasure won't last forever. Being in power won't last forever, and whoever believes it does needs to check the record of every human who was rich and powerful and see if their possessions went with them to the grave. "For we brought nothing into the world, and we cannot take anything out of the world (1 Timothy 6:7)." The old saying goes, "Never seen a U-haul behind a hearse." The lessons of History show that "Man's ingenuity often overcomes geological handicaps: he can irrigate deserts and air-condition the Sahara; he can level or surmount mountains and terrace the hills with vines; he can build a floating city to cross the ocean, or gigantic birds to navigate the sky. But a tornado can ruin in an hour the city that took a century to build; an iceberg can overturn or bisect the floating palace and send a thousand merrymakers gurgling to the Great Certainty . . . Generations of men establish a growing mastery over the earth, but they are destined to become fossils in its soil."[3]

Therefore, we should never consider selling out our God, souls, and spiritual values such as justice, righteousness, and humanity to gain anything in this fleeting world. A line should be drawn in the sand that God, our souls, and everything connected to it is off limits; it is non-negotiable. We can compromise on political and economic issues but spiritual values should never be on the table for consideration. "People can compromise, in the end, on wage increases and job security; they can pragmatically negotiate their political advantage on many public-policy issues. But God's will is something apart—it is not up for grabs or negotiable. What is sacred is sacred. What is absolute is absolute. What is eternal is eternal—at least, that is how reality can be constructed under some conditions."[4]

Unfortunately, too many Americans, especially Christians, are selling out the country and their Faith just to get into the exclusive categories only

---

3. Will & Ariel Durant, *The Lessons of History* (New York: Simon & Schuster Paperbacks, 1968), 15.

4. Christian Smith, Editor, *Disruptive Religion The Force of Faith in Social Movement Activism* (New York: Routledge Publisher, 1996), 9.

a few are in. There isn't anything wrong with making honest money and reaching a certain status as long as we don't suspend the reality of an unjust system as it relates to the poor and the desperate need for correction. We cannot imagine our way out of unjust systems; we must work our way out through constant exposure, correction, and commitment to justice and liberation. Any person, group, or organization that gives people flight into a fancy world of liberation but does not work against present unjust realities is guilty of what Karl Marx called the "Opium of the people." The opium of the people serves as a narcotic, temporarily easing the hurt and pain of the poor and oppressed in an unjust world. It is tantamount to what James stated in scripture, "What good is it, my brothers and sisters, if someone claims to have faith but has no deeds? Can such faith save them? Suppose a brother or a sister is without clothes and daily food. If one of you says to them, 'Go in peace; keep warm and well fed,' but does nothing about their physical needs, what good is it? In the same way, faith by itself, if it is not accomplished by action, is dead (James 2:17)."

Moreover, to keep the poor and the oppressed in a state of mind that keeps them from rising to correct the unjust system of which a few personally benefit is selling out the people and the Kingdom of God. When wealth and power become greater than spiritual values, it eats away at moral values; corrodes the soul; and blinds the vision of people and nations. This blindness leads to the social, economic, and political death of any nation, and to that of the postmodern church, which is supposed to be the moral and spiritual conscious of the nation. When the church ceases to lift its voice and action against structured injustice and give in to the powers that govern the neglect of the poor and oppressed, the church has sold out its spiritual heritage of the Kingdom of God and must pay a heavy price for doing so. The Bible is replete with examples of how the nation of Israel was carried off into exile for selling out its spiritual heritage and how its temples were ransacked and destroyed. When the postmodern church will pay a price for its apostasy, only time will tell. But, the fact remains when the church and its leaders fail to obey the Gospel of the Kingdom of God, the outcome is not good.

Looking back on ancient history, one cannot help but admire the young Hebrew men in the book of Daniel 3:16-18 for drawing a line in the sand concerning their God and His Kingdom. These three young men made it clear they were not going to sell out their God for a dumb idol. Although they had good positions within the Babylonian Kingdom, they were not going to sell out their souls to keep these positions. They were unwilling to bow to a system of government for which they made a living. Their Faith and souls were more important than protecting themselves within a system that kept the poor and exiles oppressed. Listen to how these three young men spoke truth to power in their determination not to sell out their souls as an example for us today:

> Shadrach, Meshach, and Abednego replied to him, 'KingNebuchadnezzar, we do not need to defend ourselves before you in this matter. If we are thrown into the blazing furnace, the God we serve can deliver us from it, and he will deliver us from Your Majesty's hand. But even if he does not, we want you to know, Your Majesty, that we will not serve your gods or worship the image of gold you have set up.

These conscientious objectors decided that the temporary material gain of anything does not compare to the worth of eternal life. They were willing to die in the fire than to live a cool life of ease and comfort. Due to the fact they were not willing to compromise their Faith and souls, they were thrown into the fiery furnace. The fire could not burn up their faith or their convictions. God saved them from the fire and ultimately won the confidence of the King that their God is God. Every occasion not to sell out may not end triumphantly as in the case of these three Hebrew men, but the principle is the same; God and the soul are not for sale.

Another example of not selling out is Queen Esther. She had become queen of the Persian Empire. Although she was in a powerful, respected position, she did not forget who she was or where she came from. The Jews were now part of the Persian Empire and history reveals that Esther did not forget nor sell out her people. She could have easily focused on her needs and kept her privileged position as a disguised Jewish Queen. But, when the Jewish people were facing genocide, she did not ignore the imminent threat but participated in its prevention. She broke a rule that could have cost her her position and life. But, she was willing to break the law and lose her life to save her people rather than enjoy the privileges of her position for a season. Sellout people only think of themselves and saving their necks, but those who have spiritual values and refuse to sell their souls are willing to face the danger and lose their physical lives if necessary for a higher spiritual cause. Esther knew what was at stake, but she resolved within herself by saying, "If I perish, I perish (Esther 4:16)." She acted on behalf of her people, and due to her brave action, the Jewish people were saved from annihilation. Esther put the needs of her people above her personal life and privileges. Think what could happen if the postmodern church puts the needs of suffering and dying people above their own political, economic, and social status and privileges.

Unfortunately, the convictions of the three Hebrew men and that of Esther did not spread across the nation of Israel. Many of the children of Israel sold out their souls and ran after other gods. They bowed down before the altars of materialism and secularism and forfeited their spiritual heritage and connection to the true and living God. They desired the glitter and glamour of worldly gain that supposedly gave them good luck, status, and importance. Many of them gained fleeting success and comfortability but were dead spiritually, as many people are today who view themselves as Christians. They had to pay a heavy price for selling out spiritual values. "Do not be deceived: God cannot be mocked. A man reaps what he sows. Whoever sows to please their flesh, from the flesh will reap destruction; whoever sows to please the Spirit, from the Spirit will reap eternal life (Galatians 6:7-8)."

There is no question we have the same problem today. Too many Christians have sold out for the world's success and comfort. They have sold out the principles and morality of the Kingdom of God to have economic and material gain. This is the reason the church remains silent when it ought to speak up. This is the reason the church has no Holy Spirit power because it prefers to accommodate the power and culture of the world. Anton Bosch stated, "Power is not measured in noise, hype, or even large numbers, just as the 'anointing' is not measured in shouting, sweat, and spit. Power cannot be measured in statistics, budgets, buildings, or programs."[5] A lot may be going on in and around a church doesn't mean that the church has Holy

---

5. Anton Bosch, "Why Is a Large Segment of the Church Powerless," *Charisma Magazine*, February 2, 2016.

Spirit power. To have Holy Spirit power means seeing the transformation of lives, people becoming disciples of Jesus Christ, and communities are transformed for the Kingdom of God. Then, we will know the Holy Spirit is at work as it was during the days of the early church. "The apostles testified powerfully to the resurrection of the Lord Jesus, and God's great blessing was upon them all. There were no needy people among them because those who owned land or houses would sell them and bring the money to the apostles to give to those in need (Acts 4:33-35)."

But, for a long time, the church has allowed itself to be lulled into the embracing tentacles of Satan—who doesn't mind giving the church a worldly stimulus to make it feel important and recognized as successful when it is a moral failure before God. Satan doesn't mind aiding and abetting the church as long as it is not engaged in transforming people and communities for the Kingdom of God. As long as the church stays out of the affairs of the state and nation and does not challenge wrong, evil, and injustice, Satan doesn't mind giving the church a few dollars, a little recognition, and a bowl of worldly pottage. As long as the church is entertaining and giving ear-tickling messages that don't convict people to repent while sprinkling a scripture or two to keep the church transactional, Satan doesn't mind endorsing such a church. For many people, the church is show time at the Apollo. Never mind if the church has no Holy Spirit power. Never mind if the Word and Power of God are not transforming souls. Never mind if the church is increasingly irrelevant to the will and purpose of the Kingdom of God. The postmodern church wants entertainment and itchy ear religion, and unless the church comes out from the sensationalism of this world, it is in danger of losing its soul and being dismissed from the presence of the Lord.

The church needs to take a new look at the life of Jesus as an example of what it ought to do when facing the temptation to sell out. When the devil showed Jesus all the Kingdoms of the world, the power and glory of them, he did so to get Jesus to sell out his ministry way before it started. The devil showed Jesus Egypt and her pharaohs; he showed Jesus Asia Minor and all of its temples; he showed him Babylon and all its palaces; he showed Jesus Rome and all her Caesars. The devil showed Jesus these kingdoms in a flash of a moment and said, "I will give them to you if you bow down and worship me (Matthew 4:8-9)." As the devil tempted Jesus to get him to bow down and worship him, many Christian men and women have bowed down themselves to get something from the devil while claiming God gave it to them. We cannot rob, cheat, and steal and claim that God gave us such things. We cannot oppress, exploit, kill, and then consign people to a paramount state of powerlessness and then say, "God bless America!" Too many Christians are involved in shady deals, corrupt policies, structural redlining, and unfair practices against the poor while singing God bless America. These people have sold out justice and righteousness to get and stay ahead.

The devil is still showing people the riches and the glamour of this world. He is busy luring people into his web of deception to get them to bow down and worship him, especially those of us who undertake to better our world, better our community, better our church, and our nation. We must remember Satan, the devil, is always there to tempt us to sell; tempt us to take the shortcut, to seek fame and glory, to get the praise of people by doing what they desire for us to do rather than doing what is right, moral and just. Just as Jesus came through every temptation, we can do the same if our hearts and priorities are right and if we have truly been spiritually born again. Jesus said to the tempter in so many words, "You better get behind me; you should worship the Lord and Him only shall you serve (Matthew 4:10)." Jesus knew the devil's tactics. He knew the devil's motives. He knew the devil's cunning ways were to get people to sell out justice, righteousness, peace, equality, and the kingdom of God. When the devil was convinced Jesus was not going to sell out to this temporary world, he left Him (Matthew 4:11)," only to return later to tempt again at another opportune time. Jesus is showing us we should never sell our spiritual heritage and heavenly home for temporary possessions and power that won't last.

A postmodern example of a man who wouldn't sell out his soul or his people is Nelson Mandela of South Africa. He was charged and convicted and spent twenty-seven years in prison fighting for justice, equality, dignity, and humanity. In prison, they did several cruel things to him, but he never gave in to the inhumane treatment he had to undergo. His convictions were stronger than his cruel conditions. His loyalty to justice was stronger than their commitment to injustice. Mandela could have easily given in and compromised the cause of justice, but it was better for him "To obey God rather than men." After twenty-seven years as a prisoner, he became President of South Africa because he would not sell his soul or the people he was fighting for. Mandela said, "During my lifetime, I have dedicated myself to this struggle of the African people. I have fought against white domination, and I have fought against black domination. I have cherished the ideal of a democratic and free society in which all persons live together in harmony and with equal opportunities. It is an ideal that I hope to live for and to achieve. But if needs be, it is an ideal for which I am prepared to die.[6] We need more leaders like this in our postmodern times to transform our world. Unfortunately, we have too many leaders: "Too hungry for status to be angry, too eager for acceptance to be bold, too self-invested in advancement to be defiant."[7]

We need not worry about our needs in this world. "God will meet all needs according to the riches of his glory in Christ Jesus (Philippians 4:19)." We don't have to sell out to the world. Never believe the saying, "When you are in Rome, act like the Romans." No, when you are in Rome, Babylon, America, etc. act like and live like children of God. Be the moral and spiritual examples for others to see. We don't have to lower and degrade ourselves to get anything from the world. We are children of God, Who knows our needs before we ask Him (Matthew 6:8)." Therefore, we don't have to sell out to sit at the table of the oppressor. We don't have to sell out the cause of Jesus Christ to go up the corporate ladder. We don't have to sell out the Kingdom of God to get a promotion. We don't have to sell out the Word of God to have friends. We don't have to sell out decency and decorum to run with the crowd. Let us stand firm in our spiritual convictions and not sell the Kingdom of God for the Kingdom of darkness. Whatever we need, our God can and will supply it. We don't have to sell our souls for a bowl of economic, social, and political pottage of this world. Benjamin Mays challenges us by making this cogent statement:

> Let it be known in your community and your profession that you are not for sale . . . that you are not putty to be molded and twisted in the

---

6. Kelsey Pelzer, Parade.com, July 18, 2023.
7. Cornel West, *Race Matters* (New York: Vintage Books, 1993), 58.

pattern of injustice and corruption. Develop strong, rock-ribbed, steel-girded characters so that whoever bumps up against you, will bounce back because they came up against a man or a woman who is not for sale . . . [8]

If enough of our leaders, politicians, pastors, parents, and citizens could stand up against wrong, evil, and injustice, we may be able to save our republic from the deep damnation it is sinking. Had not men and women, black and white, stood up against anti-democratic practices such as nazism and fascism and their manifestations, America may be in worst shape than it is today! To make America great again, not in the fashion Donald Trump has described with racist, xenophobic, and authoritarian overtones, but in the fashion of the great American reformers like Henry David Thoreau, Thomas Paine, Harriet Beecher Stowe, Harriet Tubman, Ella Baker, Fannie Lou Hamer, and others who worked for a just, fair, inclusive, and humane America. To continue this unfinished work of American reformers, we must not sell out the spiritual and democratic values and principles we hold dear as a nation. Martin Luther King, Jr.'s words are as relevant today as they were decades ago. His words are still a challenge to America:

> We as a nation must undergo a radical revolution of values. We must rapidly begin—we must rapidly begin the shift from a thing-oriented society to a person-oriented society. When machines and computers, profit motives, and property rights are considered more important than people, the giant triplets of racism, extreme materialism, and militarism are incapable of being conquered. A true revolution of values will soon cause us to question the fairness and justice of many of our past and present policies. On the one hand, we are called to play the Good Samaritan on life's roadside, but that will be only an initial act. One day, we must come to see that the whole Jericho road must be transformed so that men and women will not be constantly beaten and robbed as they make their journey on life's highway. True compassion is more than flinging a coin to a beggar. It comes to see that an edifice that produces beggars needs restructuring.

---

8. Benjamin Mays, *Walking Integrity*, 256.

Our souls, children, principals, values, nation, and future are too important to sell out to a world that is falling apart and dying from wars, weather, and wickedness. The more we sell out, the more we lose ourselves and, ultimately, our souls. The choice is ours: stand up and save the soul of America or sell out and lose the soul of the nation as well as our souls.

Chapter Six

THE NEED TO BECOME ONE NATION

> *One family, one nation, indivisible. That mentality is essential for our salvation.* —LOUIS GOSSETT, JR.

All of my life, I have pledged allegiance to the flag, saying, "One nation under God, indivisible, with liberty and justice for all." I truly believe America could be the embodiment of these words, but disappointed these words have not come to fruition since I have been saying them. "If you are black, you cannot easily join in the anthem's refrain, recite the pledge, or affirm that your country is committed to equality. While you grant that the United States is "your" country, you may define your citizenship as partial and qualified. It is not that you are "disloyal" if that means having your first allegiance elsewhere. Rather, you feel no compelling commitment to a republic that has always rebuffed you and your people."[1]

America has the potential to pledge allegiance a reality, but the practice is far from professing. As a nation, we have come a long way and have a long way to go. The original fault line that divides America by race, religion, economic, and political differences are just as de-facto now as they were at the founding of this nation. Life in America has changed, but the divisions remain the same. Out of all the social movements, the civil war,

---

1. Andrew Hacker, *Two Nations Black And White, Separate, Hostile, Unequal* (New York: Ballantine Books, 1992, 1995), 52.

the civil rights struggle, and the loss of life to create one nation, we are still a deeply divided country.

To make matters worse, our state and national governments are driving a wider wedge between the citizenry, causing the nation's division to become more acute. Anytime division cannot be bridged for the common good, enemies, both foreign and domestic, take advantage of this vulnerability. To protect ourselves now and in the near future, we must become "One nation, under God, indivisible, with liberty and justice for all."

The reason America is falling short of becoming one nation is we deal with the symptoms of our divisions but never the causes. Putting a Band-Aid on our deep divisions is not going to heal nor bridge the chasm. Blue states and red states have metastasized to the point that political violence is now in the equation of our division. What happened to disagreeing without becoming disagreeable? Until America acknowledges the causes of these divisions and works to correct them, the country can claim but never be, in reality, a nation of "American exceptionalism." Kevin Phillips stated, "This national self-importance is no secret, at home or abroad. For centuries Americans have believed themselves special, a people and nation chosen by God to play a unique and even redemptive role in the world. Elected leaders tend to proselytize and promote this exceptionalism—presidential inaugural addresses are a frequent venue—without appending the necessary historical cautions."[2] Promoting American exceptionalism without practicing it at home is delusional at best. Salem Al Suwaidi stated, "The only thing exceptional about America is that it has conceptualized its identity as a state of freedom and equality while simultaneously building the nation through mass displacement and genocide . . . American Exceptionalism' is essentially an over-exaggeration of the history of the independence a group of English Colonialists gained when settling abroad and establishing the United States . . . the most exceptional element of American political history is merely that it was the first to write, boldly on paper, that it would be "free and equal," but was it the first to truly, exceptionally, apply that philosophy? Is it currently applying that philosophy?"[3]

2. Kevin Phillips, *American Theocracy The Peril And Politics of Radical Religion, Oil, and Borrowed Money in the 21st Century,* (New York: Penguin Publishing Group, 2006), 125.

3. Salem Al Suwaidi, "Is 'American Exceptionalism' A Myth?" *Dialogue & Discourse,* November 4, 2020.

The creeds and deeds of American ideas of freedom, justice, and democracy have not come together. A lot of conversation takes place, but the commitment to resolve the causes of our division is glossed over. Conversation, conferences, seminars, worship, and prayer meetings have their place, but unless actions accompany these things with legislation, what good have they served? God never said, "Let worship, prayer, conferences, and seminars roll down like waters." God said, "Let justice roll down like waters and righteousness like a mighty stream (Amos 5:24)." Unless justice is meted out across this nation from the top to the bottom, America cannot survive as a democracy. As people of goodwill fought to save the union in the 19th century, this same commitment must be employed today to save democracy and the freedoms guaranteed under the law.

The idea of being different, unique, and a symbol of liberty and democracy may be the nation's goal, but in practice, the nation continues to fall short. Unresolved issues like racism, injustice, inequality, police brutality, mass incarceration, immigration, etc., keep the nation from being what it claims to be at home and around the world. These issues have not been resolved, and until they are, America's credibility is questionable. Many of our national leaders tap dance around these issues, kicking the can down to the next congress and senate, further dividing the nation. This is the reason several justice issues have not been enacted. Our legislators are refusing to come together for the good of the nation, keeping the nation divided without understanding that if America falls, they will fall along with it.

Too often, America gets caught up in other concerns that divert its attention away from these perennial issues, and the division in the nation remains. The present existential threat in America is not terrorism but our deep economic, social, and political divisions that are getting wider year after year. Ignoring our deep divisions causes them to fester, and we are worse off as a result. The cancer of division is eating away at our republic, and these unresolved issues are bringing us closer to national demise. The truth hurts, but we must face these issues to fix them. When the desires of special interests are met over the unmet common interests of the people, this weakens democracy to the point that it has to be put in the hospital to survive. It is no secret that American democracy is in intensive care, hooked up to a life support system. Unless we provide critical care to our democracy, it will die due to benign neglect. Henry Nelson Wieman reminded us years ago about the potential dangers to democracy:

> Private interests are precious because they express the needs of localities, groups, and individuals who are truly different from one another. These must be expressed and satisfied as far as possible. But these diverse and changing demands must not be allowed to obstruct the action required to defend and strengthen what sustains them. Zeal for the golden eggs must not kill the goose that lays them. The struggle of each unique individual, each unique locality, each unique business organization, or other organized group to get the special kind of golden egg it needs or wants will kill the goose unless some agency cares for the goose. The unsolved problem of democracies is to untie the hands of government at the top level so that they can care for the goose. Democracy and freedom cannot be saved unless we restore to democratic government the power to govern.[4]

The aristocracy controls the American government at the top level, and unless the American government is freed from top-level interest groups, democracy could die an untimely death. Unless we truly have a government of the people, by the people, and for the people, there is no chance for democracy to survive. The future state of the nation is dependent upon the will of the people. If we, the people, allow ourselves to continue to be manipulated by the aristocracy at the top, whatever the outcome of the nation is can only be laid at our feet. "If democracy and freedom are to be saved, these are the two requirements: Demonstrable truth concerning the common good which underlies and sustains the diversity of local and private interests but not identical with any part or whole of them; secondly, a form of religion which leads people to trust and commit themselves to the common good sufficiently to allow their governments to command resources and concerted action in its service independently of local and private interests."[5]

Over time, we have allowed money and power to speak louder than the common good of the people. To protect themselves from the masses

---

4. Henry Nelson Wieman, *Creative Freedom Vocation of Liberal Religion*, edited by Creighton Peden and Larry E. Axel (New York: The Pilgrim Press, 1982), 83–84.

5. Ibid., 86.

of common people due to a broken system, the rich and powerful give to charities, but this doesn't achieve social and economic justice. Power is still protected by the powerful. Joel Edward Goza stated, "Benevolence does what it is designed to do—ease the conscience of the powerful and empty the gratitude of the powerless to reinforce a broken social order. Though historically private benevolence proves a superficial solution to suffering resulting from public, systemic failures, superficial solutions rarely fail to satisfy the wealthy."[6] Unless we fix the broken system that keeps the poor and working class marginalized, we are on the cusp of another Civil War. We survived the first Civil War; it is unlikely we will survive the next one. Due to advanced theology and militarization, America could wipe itself out within a matter of days. When people get to the place they don't have anything to lose, "Society dissolves into nothing more than contending factions, as the Founding Fathers of America understood so well—a war of all against all."[7] The Founding Fathers put in place guard rails to maintain democracy, but when these guard rails are ignored, lawlessness ensues. Not that the Founding Fathers were perfect; for they were conflicted men. "If there is anything to learn from the Founding Fathers, it's that we have the right to call out tyranny by its name and transform our society. But we don't have to remain enslaved to the limited moral imaginations of those who rationalized slavery and genocide. We can dream better, more inclusive dreams and create a more just society."[8] To bring about this just society, we must repent and become one nation and "Do justly, love mercy, and walk humbly with God (Micah 6:8)."

People ask are we really on the cusp of a civil war? The answer is a resounding yes. "The democratization of abundance—the expectation that each generation would enjoy a standard of living beyond the reach of its predecessors—has given way to a reversal in which age-old inequalities are beginning to reestablish themselves, sometimes at a frightening rate, sometimes so gradually as to escape notice."[9] Who can deny January 6, 2021, when Americans believed the election was stolen? The results of the 2024 election could be the start of an all-out war of Americans against

---

6. Joel Edward Goza, *America's Unholy Ghosts The Racists Roots of Our Faith and Politics* (Eugene, OR: Cascade Books, 2019), 136.

7. Christopher Lasch, *The Revolt of the Elites And the Betrayal of Democracy,* 49.

8. Crystal M. Fleming, *How To Be Less Stupid About Race* (Boston: Beacon Press, 2018), 48.

9. Ibid., 30.

themselves. We can no longer talk about one nation! It is either one nation or no nation at all. "When freedom is understood to be the total unified self in action in such a way as to realize progressively the constructive potentialities of each human being. Therefore we cannot be free if we tolerate conditions, practices, and attitudes which seriously hinder the appreciative understanding of one another."[10]

Chris Vance points out where we stand today as a nation and how America is still very divided. "On one side stands the well-educated and well-off, those that are prospering in this new economy. On the other stands the working class, which often struggles against the effects of automation and the loss of traditional high-wage manufacturing jobs. We are becoming two nations divided by economics, values, and culture. The division is also taking place against the backdrop of our longstanding racial inequalities."[11]

Ben Carson believes the unity of the nation is not going to come by osmosis. Every American must take an active role in changing the nation and learn the lessons of the past:

> We need to take an active role in changing the course of our nation if we are to live up to the motto "one nation under God, indivisible, with liberty and justice for all." We are the pinnacle nation in the world right now, but if the examples of Egypt, Greece, Rome, and Great Britain teach us anything, it is that pinnacle nations are not guaranteed their place forever. If we fail to rediscover the basic principles of common sense, manners, and morality, we will go the same way they did. Fortunately, our downward pathway is not an inexorable one. It is not too late to learn from the mistakes of those who preceded us and take the kinds of corrective action that will ensure a promising future for those who come after us.[12]

The question is how can we become one nation, and what broad steps do we have to take? To heal a problem, we must first have an accurate diagnosis before applying the right therapy. The major problem in America is its foundation. The social, economic, and political structures that were

---

10. Henry Nelson Wieman, *Creative Freedom*, 22.
11. Chris Vance, "America Needs a 'One Nation,'" niskanencenter.org, June 25, 2020.
12. Ben Carson, *One Nation: What We Can Do to Save America's Future* (New York: Sentinel, 2014), 3.

built did not have the poor and the oppressed at the table. The poor and the oppressed had no say in how the nation would be structured. Those who structured the nation were white men who were the key architects that arranged society in a hierarchy of which they assigned themselves at the top having power, privilege, prosperity, and protection. From this top tier, the 4 p's would flow down to the rest of the country. The problem with this is the 4 p's never flowed down to the middle and lower classes of people. This enormous gap created almost 250 years ago is the major problem with why America has remained a divided nation and why it is hard to protect democracy when justice and equality are still not a reality with all the inhabitants of this land. When life, liberty, and the pursuit of happiness have been undermined by racism, sexism, and oppression, unity and patriotism are difficult to embrace now since DEI Diversity, Inclusion, and Diversity have been stripped away in the federal and private sectors.

Furthermore, when the rich are getting richer and the poor are becoming poorer, this shows the system constructed by the founding fathers works for the top one percent but does not work for those trapped at the bottom. Intentional or unintentional, this is the way it is in America. Until America faces the fact that systematic unfairness is alive and well and repents and corrects this fundamental problem, the nation cannot become one.

America must face the fact that slavery made this nation a superpower by setting it on a trajectory to be prosperous when it didn't have to pay for labor for over two and half centuries. Non-payment to the slaves created a permanent underclass that is still in place today. The descendants of slaves are still devoid of justice, equality, and economic access. Black Americans had no rights, justice, or freedom, whereas whites were bound to respect for centuries. It took a civil war, civil rights struggle, and the deaths of many blacks and whites to gain basic rights for American citizens. Until America repents of its original sins and their manifestations, becoming one nation is not possible. Repentance means to acknowledge the sin, regret it, and start to finish the work of healing and repairing the damage done. Some may say that America has repented from slavery, but where is the evidence that America has made the social and economic commitment to repair the damage done by slavery? Why hasn't America given black people reparations, which we will discuss further in the next chapter, like it has done for other ethnic groups like the Jews, the Japanese, and Native Americans, etc? Releasing the slaves to be free is a start, but what about their descendants becoming slaves to society when social, economic, and educational injustices and inequalities are still realities for them? The same system that was predicated upon racism and oppression is still not transformed to level the playing field.

For centuries, racism has blocked opportunities for black people, and it is still deeply rooted in the black community. The American government has confirmed this through a study done by the National Advisory Commission on Civil Disorder, which is the backdrop of our longstanding racial inequalities Chris Vance mentioned in his statement. The Kerner report said:

> Our nation is moving toward two societies, one black, and one white—
> separate and unequal. Racial prejudice, discrimination, and segregation
> have shaped our history decisively; they now threaten the future of every
> American. Why did it happen? Certain fundamental matters are clear.
> Of these, the most fundamental is the racial attitude and behavior of
> white Americans toward black Americans . . . White racism is essentially
> responsible . . . What white Americans have fully understood, but what
> [black people] can never forget—is that white society is deeply implicated
> in the ghetto. White institutions created it, white institutions maintained
> it, and white society condones it.[13]

It would be wonderful if the American government did a study on how to correct the wrong done to black people to become one nation. It doesn't make sense black people have fought in every American war to help make America free, a democracy, and a superpower, and then they cannot be treated with justice, dignity, and humanity! It is one thing to state the problem but quite another to remedy it. To become one nation, we have to face what is preventing it. The great prevention is racial injustice, greed, and white supremacy, and unless America is willing to delete these practices and ideologies from its national life, becoming one nation cannot happen. Andrew Hacker stated the reason black people are behind in the social,

---

13. National Advisory Commission on Civil Disorder, U. S. Government Printing Office, 1968, 1.

economic, and educational life of the nation and is directly linked to their history of slavery and oppression. He puts this challenge before America:

> It is white America that has made being black so disconsolate an estate. Legal slavery may be in the past, but segregation and subordination have been allowed to persist. Even today, America imposes a stigma on every black child at birth. . . . A huge racial chasm remains, and there are few signs that the coming century will see it closed. A century and a quarter after slavery, white America continues to ask of its black citizens an extra patience and perseverance that whites have never required of themselves. So the question for white Americans is essentially moral: is it right to impose on members of an entire race a lesser start in life and then to expect from them a degree of resolution that has never been demanded from your race?[14]

To become one nation, the question that Andrew Hacker has posed must be answered not just with words but by legislative policies to become the law of the land. Up until now, the question remains unanswered. The American people and their politicians cannot keep on kicking the can down to the next Congress and Senate. Our nation does not have much time to face and fix this problem. We either face and fix it now or be destroyed by it later. Do we want one America or continue to take our chances with two Americas, as Martin Luther King, Jr. described?

> There are two Americas. One America is beautiful for situation. In this America, millions of people have the milk of prosperity and the honey of equality flowing before them. This America is the habitat of millions of people who have food and material necessities for their bodies, culture, education for their minds, freedom, and human dignity for their spirits. In this America, children grow up in the sunlight of opportunity. But there is another America. This other America has a daily ugliness about it that transforms the buoyancy of hope into the fatigue of despair. In this other America, . . . millions of people are forced to live in distressing housing conditions . . . So the vast majority of [blacks] in America find themselves

---

14. Andrew Hacker, *Two Nations Black And White, Separate, Hostile, Unequal*, 245.

perishing on an island of poverty in the midst of a vast ocean of material prosperity. This has caused a great deal of bitterness. It has caused ache and anguish . . . These conditions are the things that cause individuals to feel that they don't have any other alternative than to engage in violent rebellions to get attention. And I must say tonight that a riot is the language of the unheard. And what is it America has failed to hear? It has failed to hear that the plight of the [black] poor has worsened over the last twelve or fifteen years. It has failed to hear that the promises of freedom and justice have not been met . . . we will never solve the problem of racism until there is a recognition of the fact that racism still stands at the center of so much of our nation, and we must see racism for what it is.[15]

Until America stops practicing racism and corrects the injustices against the poor and the oppressed, riots, mayhem, and unrest shall be its constant companions. America is already top-heavy with gun violence, police brutality, and an overcrowded prison population. These social malaises are only going to increase in varicosity and intensity, with no one feeling safe. We know there is a direct correlation between forced injustice and poverty that creates an unsafe society. Amos Wilson said, "The black lower class is caught in the most vicious cycle of all. Due to racism, economic, social, political, and educational discrimination, it has been pushed into a position of powerlessness . . . The refusal of the larger society to effectively invest money and resources in the low-income communities (actually, there is a tendency to disinvest in these communities), coupled with overcrowdedness and low extension motivation of the black underclass, produces what are aptly called slums."[16] Slums produce dysfunctional behavior and criminality in an effort to survive hopelessness and powerlessness, which impact the safety of the larger society.

To combat marginalization that creates an unsafe society, Henry Nelson Wieman suggested demonstrable truth for the common good coupled with a religious commitment that wields great influence on those in positions of responsibility. What Wieman suggested could work, but the present religion

15. Martin Luther King, Jr., *The Other America*, http://www.ghhistorical.org/mlk/index.htm, Grosse Point High School on March 14, 1968.

16. Amos Wilson, *The Developmental Psychology of The Black Child* (New York: Africana Research Publication, 1978), 176.

in America cannot be utilized. Religion, especially White Christianity in America, must make a radical transformation of its present complicity with oppression and must also untie itself from racism and white supremacy. Jemar Tisby stated, "Christianity in America has been tied to the fallacy of white supremacy for hundreds of years. European colonists brought with them ideas of white supremacy and paternalism toward darker-skinned people. On this sandy foundation, they erected a society and a version of religion that could only survive through the subjugation of people of color. Minor repairs by the weekend-warrior racial reconcilers won't fix a flawed foundation. The church needs the Carpenter from Nazareth to deconstruct the house that racism built and remake it into a house for all nations."[17] White Christianity is not in line with the Kingdom of God as long as it remains tied to the white power structure. Tony Evans said, "For too long, Christians have wrapped the Christian faith in the American flag, often creating a civil religion and an illegitimate Christian nationalism that falsely equates politics with the Kingdom of God. This is foreign to the way God intended His church to function."[18]

Sadly, white Christianity in America gave birth to white supremacy. Its ongoing complicity in the subjugation of people of color is morally wrong. Jeannine Hill Fletcher stated, "Good White Christian friends do not see very clearly the way the disparity and injustice we experience today has been legislated by the United States since the beginning of its history . . . Many may recognize vaguely that our current conditions are the result of generational dispossessions . . . If good White Christians want to see changes in the world toward racial harmony, they must work for racial justice. Justice will not come from individual acts of charity but will require the transformation of our social structures. Transforming unjust social structures is not their problem alone, but ours together . . . White supremacy grew from a dangerous ideology to an accepted subject position inherited by Whites. The systems and structures of white supremacy have been intimately joined with Christian supremacy, such that undoing white

---

17. Jemar Tisby, *The Color of Compromise The Truth About The American Church's Complicity in Racism* (Grand Rapids, MI: Zondervan, 2019), 24.

18. Tony Evans, *Oneness Embraced A Kingdom Race Theology For Reconciliation Unity And Justice* (Chicago: Moody Publisher, 2022), 13.

supremacy will also require relinquishing the ideologies and theologies of Christian supremacy."[19]

Since White Christianity is tied to white supremacy, it cannot be considered a mature religion to fit Wieman's description of what is needed to bring unity and save freedom and democracy. White Christianity's track record is too unjust, biased, and discriminatory and has done too much damage to God's children in their efforts to maintain white supremacy. White Christians must be willing to give up white Christianity that sustains white supremacy for the Christianity of Christ. The Christianity of Christ is love, justice, forgiveness, and the Kingdom of God. To embrace one feature while neglecting other features is denying the Christianity of Christ. We cannot cherry-pick what feature to embrace without making the whole inauthentic. Most Christians pick the forgiveness feature and leave the others undone. Jesus Christ said, "No one can serve two masters; Either you will hate the one and love the other, or you will be devoted to the one and despise the other. You cannot serve both God and money (Matthew 6:24)." Until White Christianity switches its master of white supremacy to the Master of Jesus Christ, it stands in the way of solving our racial problems and creating a new America of liberty and justice for all.

To have justice for all, an understanding of racism and oppression must be understood by the dominant group and how they are complicit in it. Too many good white people don't have a clue how racism works and the ongoing damage it does to its victims. Jane Elliott, a white teacher from Iowa, understands how white supremacy and racism have muddied the waters of racial justice, equality, and democracy. For more than five decades, she has been on the battlefield telling the truth about the unfair racial practices against people of color:

> I think white people aren't aware that racism isn't just wearing white hoods and burning crosses. It's also fixing the system so that black votes don't get counted. It's refusing to open the polling places in precincts where most of the eligible voters are people of color. It's outlawing affirmative action at the state level, even though it has proven successful.

19. Jeannine Hill Fletcher, *The Sin of White Supremacy, Christianity, Racism, & Religious Diversity in America* (Maryknoll, NY: Orbis Books, 2017), 8–9, 15.

It's building more prisons than we build schools and guaranteeing that they will be filled by targeting young men of color with things like the "three strikes" legislation in California and the DWB—"driving while black." These are problems encountered by young black men all over this country. It's the fact that there are more children attending segregated schools in the US today than there were previous to *Brown v. Board of Education*. It's white flight and red-lining by financial institutions. It's television programing that portrays people of color as villains and white people as their victims. It's ballot-security systems that are used to intimidate minority voters and so result in the very activities which they are supposedly designed to prevent.[20]

This is the national cancer America has to acknowledge and cure if freedom and democracy are to be saved in this nation. To ignore this cancer diagnosis is to condemn the republic to death.

To return to Henry Nelson Wieman's explanation of what else is needed to save freedom and democracy, he points out the economy and how it must be predicated upon fairness to the working class and its accessibility to them. Too often, the economy helps the rich get richer while the poor working class struggles to get ahead. Christopher Lasch made the point that as time goes on, both the poor and the middle class will be affected by economic inequality as cities across the nation continue to swell. "As the collapse of civic life in these swollen cities continues, not only the poor but the middle classes will experience conditions unimaginable a few years ago. Middle-class standards of living can be expected to decline throughout what is all too hopefully referred to as the developing world."[21]

Therefore, it behooves us to consider Wieman's three social developments. The first of these developments is the economy. Wieman suggests that the economy must work for all. The wealth generated from mass production and automation should provide the increasing ability for the workers to purchase what is produced. "These forms of production require great concentration of wealth controlled by a few but at the same time a very great distribution of wealth in the hands of many. Not only must there be a

---

20. "An Unfinished Crusade: An Interview with Jane Elliott," *PBS Frontline*, January 1, 2023.

21. Christopher Lasch, *The Revolt of the Elites And The Betrayal of Democracy,* 30–31.

WE NEED EACH OTHER

wide distribution of material wealth but also a wide distribution of education and cultural privilege because otherwise, the many highly equipped minds needed to operate industry will not be available. Also, without education and culture, abundant consumption will be destructive."[22] Wieman further believes if education and religion are coupled with a developing economy, social justice could arise.

The second social development is political. Wieman states that this includes government and all organizations to share in the exercise of power. "The power of the mightiest in the society now developing is sustained and increased by continually increasing the power of the many. The many different agencies of power under the responsible control of many different people must all work together if a few are to have supreme power. In a society as complex as ours and now becoming worldwide, power and responsibility must be very widely distributed because no small group can operate all the innumerable and diverse organizations of power, each of which is necessary to sustain the power of all the others and therefore also the power of those at the highest levels of control."[23] Wieman goes on to explain that the social revolution around the world makes conflict inevitable. When it comes to wealth, power, and distribution, it is creating a dangerous world in which there must be a mediator of mature religion as the third social development.

The third social development is managing the conflict that ultimately comes from warring powers. Communism and capitalism conflict and this conflict poses a threat to humanity. Both economic and social systems are distributing wealth, power, and culture to win the world to its side. However, unless a mature religion can create a kind of appreciative understanding of both sides, the very survival of humanity is at stake. Wieman stated:

> Nothing is more important than the kind of interchange that creates
> appreciative understanding across the barriers of diverse cultures, faiths,
> social systems, races, and economic and political interests. The day has
> come for the kind of religion that directs the ultimate commitment of
> humankind to the creativity that transforms the mind in this way. This

---

22. Henry Nelson Wieman, *Creative Freedom*, 101.
23. Ibid., 102.

is the day of its opportunity and the day of its saving power if it will rise to the challenge. The great transition is upon us from widespread poverty to universal abundance, from warring peoples to a world community, from international anarchy to a level of existence more gracious and understanding of human need than the past has ever known. The transition will either destroy us or be consummated. Religion carries the heaviest load of responsibility for deciding which it will be.[24]

To bring a divided nation together to save our democracy, we must heavily consider the Brooking findings:

We cannot be united states if we have separate economies, with wealthy elites living in penthouses high above struggling streets or coastal states surging ahead and interior states falling behind. America needs to find a leader who can unite the nation around a plan for economic growth that spreads outside of the cities and includes everyone. Economists call efforts to address vertical inequality "people-based" policies and efforts to address horizontal inequality "place-based" policies. A new national economic strategy combining both approaches would have broad support and would bring greater inclusiveness and opportunity to the people and places in America that have been falling behind.[25]

The salvation of our nation is up to us. We can lay aside our differences and put justice and country first, or continue to fight and devour one another as fools. The American ship of democracy has hit an iceberg and water is pouring into the ship. The top deck of the ship is in as much danger as the lower deck of the ship. Unless we become one nation and stop the water from flowing into the American ship, it will sink. It won't matter about our social, economic, political, class, and cultural differences. We will perish, and the rest of the world will say, "Oh, how the mighty have fallen." Abraham Lincoln warned us more than a century ago, "America will never be destroyed from the outside. If we falter and lose our freedoms,

---

24. Ibid., 103.
25. Brookings.edu, "To unite a divided nation, we must tackle both vertical and horizontal inequality," Alice M. Rivlin, Allan Rivlin, and Sheri Rivlin, November 5, 2019.

it will be because we destroyed ourselves." Jewel Medley expanded on Lincoln's warning to America:

> Lincoln asserted that America's demise could only come from within. Perhaps he believed that the corruption of the policies of the economy and government could bring us to our knees. This prophetic knowledge has proven accurate in modern times. Avarice in enterprise at the expense of the common citizen has caused the American political climate to trend away from true democracy, where the majority is no longer represented, and the ideals of pluralism and majoritarianism are lost. When large, powerful corporations control media, money, and government, an irresolvable conflict of interest occurs in which the few control the many.[26]

As we move forward in this 21st Century, America must understand that she is no stronger than her weakest link. Until we stop fighting and labeling one another to shut down conversations that are not comfortable, we cannot unite our divided nation. Ben Carson makes a very cogent appeal:

> If we are to survive as a united nation, we must learn how to engage in civil discussion of our differences without becoming bitter enemies. We cannot fall for the Saul Alinsky trick of not having a conversation while trying to demonize each other. Let's talk about the tough issues without scrutinizing every word and castigating anyone who dares to violate the PC rules. There is nothing wrong with disagreement—in fact, if two people talk about everything, one of them isn't necessary. I believe we are all necessary so let's toss out the hypersensitivity and roll up our sleeves and start working together to solve our problems.[27]

---

26. Jewel Medley, "Abraham Lincoln Predicted U.S. Downfall by Avarice," *The Thinker*, May 28, 2017, https://essayfrolic.wordpress.com/2017/05/28/.

27. Ben Carson, *One Nation: What We Can Do to Save America's Future*, 24.

Chapter Seven

THE COST OF RECONCILIATION

> *Reconciliation should be accompanied by justice; otherwise, it will not last. While we all hope for peace, it shouldn't be peace at any cost but peace based on principle, on justice."*
> —CORAZON AQUINO

We have been doing a lot of talk about reconciliation, and that's all it ends up being is talk. Over the years, we have talked about forgiveness and reconciliation, but the power dynamic between the forgivers and the forgiven remains the same. This power dynamic of the forgiven group holding a surplus of power while the forgiver group still suffers from a deficit of power poses a problem for the oppressed group. If the forgiven group does not right the wrong done to the forgiver group, how can reconciliation come about? If justice is not the start and outcome of reconciliation, it is no reconciliation at all. Reconciliation is more than talk, more than conferences and seminars. If we are serious about reconciliation, it entails work; it entails sacrifice and cost. America is lacking in all three, and this is the reason the power dynamic has not changed. We love to talk about reconciliation, but when the rubber hits the road, America doesn't want to pay the cost.

Although black people have been robbed of humanity, exploited of their wages, denied economic opportunities, lynched and burned, and blown to pieces by the smoking guns of white supremacy for over 400 years, it is amazing how America can give billions of dollars to foreign countries but cannot right the wrong done to black people on its American soil. The hypocrisy is financing democracy abroad but refusing to finance it at home. How can the American government agree to give foreign aid to people who have not been enslaved, pillaged, exploited, or discriminated against on this American soil, yet earmarked money goes to foreign countries while black people are still suffering from the effects of liabilities incurred during and after slavery? The question is not how but when will America make amends to black people who laid the economic floor of this nation to become a superpower? How long must a people wait to receive justice from a nation of which they have given their all to be treated with appreciation? America talks about justice and democracy as the touchstone of its republic. This talk rings in the ears of black people with piercing familiarity. But, no commitment is made to correct the historical wrongs done to black people. All types of excuses are given not to give reparations to black people, and some blame the victims for their plight in America.

However, reparation or restitution is a Biblical concept that reveals the mind of God, especially when death, injury, and loss are involved. Leviticus 6:4-5 it says, "You must give back whatever you stole, or the money you took by extortion, or the security deposit, or the lost property you found, or anything obtained by swearing falsely. You must make restitution by paying the full price plus an additional 20 percent to the person you have harmed (NLT)." Of course, this is the Old Testament, but what about reparation or restitution in the New Testament? In Luke 19:8-9 it says, "But Zacchaeus stood up and said to the Lord, "Look, Lord! Here and now, I give half of my possessions to the poor, and if I have cheated anybody out of anything, I will pay back four times the amount." Jesus said to him, "Today, salvation has come to this house because this man, too, is a son of Abraham." How long will America delay its salvation? We can look past this historical injustice and forget the debt that is owed, but God cannot. "Vengeance is Mine, I will repay, says the Lord (Romans 12:19)."

How would you feel to labor and see the fruits of your labor going to others while you are overlooked and denied the fruits of your labor? America has paid reparations to previous slave owners, Native Americans,

Japanese Americans, and Jews who have received billions of dollars, land, and other benefits, but black America is still given what Martin Luther King, Jr. called "A bad check, a check which has come back marked 'insufficient funds.' But we refuse to believe that the bank of justice is bankrupt."[1] Here it is four hundred years later, and black people have not received their 40 acres and a mule. The constant delay in giving black people justice is the moral shame of America. Other groups are given reparations, acceptance, and approval for life, liberty, and the pursuit of happiness, and many of these people dare to tell black people to get over slavery and then move to talk about reconciliation without compensation! They don't understand no justice, no reconciliation!

Black Americans are the only group that has not received reparations for state-sanctioned racial discrimination, while slavery afforded some white families the ability to accrue tremendous wealth. And we must note that American slavery was particularly brutal. About 15 percent of the enslaved shipped from Western Africa died during transport. The enslaved were regularly beaten and lynched for frivolous infractions. Slavery also disrupted families as one in three marriages were split up, and one in five children were separated from their parents. The case for reparations can be made on economic, social, and moral grounds. The United States had multiple opportunities to atone for slavery—each a missed chance to make the American Dream a reality—but has yet to undertake significant action.[2]

It was not right then, and it is not right now! Unless people of goodwill come together and make reparation a national concern as it has done with Roe vs Wade, gun legislation, woke, and other national concerns, it is unlikely that we will ever achieve reconciliation. It is shameful before God that since James Forman made the case for reparation at the Riverside Church in New York City in 1969, it has not gotten much traction in implementation to this day. A few congressional leaders have started to entertain reparations since the George Floyd killing in 2020, but there is still no legislative bill waiting for the President to sign to be enacted as law in the land. Martin Luther King Jr said, "Justice too long delayed is

---

1. Martin Luther King, Jr. "I Have A Dream Speech," Lincoln Memorial March on Washington, August 1963.

2. Brookings, "Why We Need Reparations For Black Americans," Rashawn Ray and Andre M. Perry, April 15, 2020, brookings.edu

justice denied."[3] This speaks volumes that neither the white church nor the government both complicit in the social, economic, and psychological injury of black people and their descendants are serious about reconciliation. Black people are not asking for welfare but justice, and reparations are due to them because of the injury done to them as a people. The wealth gap between blacks and whites is the direct result of the legacy of slavery and discrimination. Freeing black people from slavery was not enough. President Lyndon B Johnson understood this when he said these words:

> In far too many ways, American Negroes have been another nation: deprived of freedom, crippled by hatred, the doors of opportunity closed to hope . . . Freedom is not enough. You do not wipe away the scars of centuries by saying: Now you are free to go where you want, and do as you desire, and choose the leaders you please. You do not take a person who, for years, has been hobbled by chains and liberate him, bring him up to the starting line of a race and then say, "You are free to compete with all the others," and still believe you have been completely fair . . . For the task is to give 20 million Negroes the same chance as every other American to learn and grow, to work and share in society, to develop their abilities—physical, mental and spiritual, and to pursue their happiness. To this end equal opportunity is essential, but not enough, not enough.[4]

President Johnson understood that without giving black people back their stolen wages for wealth-building opportunities, freedom was not enough when they were still slaves to society socially, economically, and educationally. More must be done or otherwise, racial reconciliation is not possible.

It is amazing how good white Christians can read the story of Zacchaeus in Luke 19:1-9 and not understand this story deals with giving back what was ill-gotten. Many white ministers talk about Zacchaeus' effort to get to Jesus but not what was done after Zacchaeus fellowshipped with Jesus. Dodging what Zacchaeus said to Jesus, "Look, Lord! Here and now I give half of my possessions to the poor, and if I have cheated anybody

---

3. Martin Luther King, Jr. "Letter from Birmingham Jail," 1963.
4. Lyndon B Johnson, "To Fulfill These Rights," Commencement Address at Howard University, June 4, 1965.

out of anything, I will pay back four times the amount," is not a serious concern about reconciliation. There is a cost to reconciliation, whether we want to admit it or not.

Reparation is a part of the Gospel message. Zacchaeus knew well the necessity for repayment as an essential ingredient in repentance. 'If I have taken anything from any man by false accusation, I restore him fourfold" (Luke 19:8). The church which calls itself the servant church must, like its Lord, be willing to strip itself of possessions in order to build and restore that which has been destroyed by the compromising bureaucrats and conscienceless rich. While reparations cannot remove the guilt created by the despicable deed of slavery, it is, nonetheless, a positive response to the need for power in the black community.[5]

Jesus Christ is waiting to say to America, as was said to Zacchaeus, who was willing to pay back with interest, "Today salvation has come to this house (Luke 19:9)." There can be no salvation and no reconciliation in America until justice is done through repayment to the injured.

We cannot separate sacrifice and cost from reconciliation, especially when injustice, injury, exploitation, and economics are integral parts of the equation. Reconciliation is the basic concept of making amends to account for the wrong done, repair the damage caused, and correct the evil and injustice that fuel it. Reconciliation does not come before justice; it is on the other of justice. This means we have to do the work to achieve reconciliation and to do the work means sacrifice and cost. If there is a breakdown in terms of the cost of reconciliation, America is not serious about it. It's going to cost time, resources, and sacrifice, and if we are not willing to do this to obtain reconciliation, then we need to stop talking about reconciliation. Thomas Shapiro said, "We can no longer ignore tremendous wealth inequities as we struggle with the thorny issue of racial inequality. Without attending to how equal opportunity or even equal achievement does not lead to equal results—especially concerning wealth—we will continue to repeat the deep and disturbing patterns of racial inequality and conflict that plague our republic."[6]

5. Committee on Theological Prospectus, National Committee of Black Churchmen (NCBC), June 13, 1969.

6. Thomas M. Shapiro, *The Hidden Cost of Being African American: How Wealth Perpetuates Inequality* (Oxford: Oxford University Press, 2004), 204.

With a two-category system of rich and poor, power and powerless, oppressor and oppressed, the question is, what does reconciliation look like? If there has never been a relationship between the oppressed and oppressor, what are we reconciling to? Reconciliation presupposes that there was a previous relationship between the two groups, and this relationship was severed, causing a separation. Therefore, reconciliation means taking the necessary steps to get back to the previous relationship. But, the problem is the previous relationship between the oppressed and oppressor has never been based upon justice and equality. Again, the question is, what are we reconciling to? Reconciliation cannot mean returning to a superior and inferior situation; which means we must admit there was never a relationship based upon justice, equality, and mutual respect between the oppressed and oppressor groups. What we can do is form a new relationship not based upon a previous assumption there was a relationship to reconcile to. Reconciliation means creating a new relationship with the understanding that justice should be our point of departure. Then, this new relationship should include taking responsibility for correcting the socioeconomic political gains during the old forced interaction between the oppressed and oppressor. Both groups must play their parts to bring about fundamental transformation to both groups. But, let there be no misunderstanding that to achieve reconciliation, there is a significant price tag.

The late Rosemary Ruether, a famed female theologian, understands the complexity of achieving reconciliation. She believes reconciliation must include in the process a deconstruction of the dominant ideology that normalizes sin and injustice.

> The critical question for any discussion of reconciliation is, how does one nurture the growth of a breakthrough community of friends that crosses boundaries, deconstructs the dominant ideology that normalizes sin and injustice, and shapes an alternative praxis of mutuality that can touch and transform both personal consciousness and social structures? This is not easy. The pathway to conversion, transformation and justice that grounds reconciliation is filled with pitfalls. But the first step is taken when persons across broken relations glimpse one another as friends, and are no longer able to affirm themselves without affirming the other at the same

time. In other words, the ground and fruits of conversion is love, for it is love that melts the heart of stone and gives us hearts of flesh by which we begin to experience what it means to love the neighbor as oneself.[7]

However, before we get to reconciliation and peace, there must first be repentance. Too often we want reconciliation without true repentance that starts the process for real reconciliation. If America cannot confess her original sin of slavery, oppression, exploitation, discrimination, and today's systemic racism and have the willingness to repent from this perennial problem, there is no true start toward real reconciliation. Having kumbaya flashes in the pan programs that maintain a power imbalance that results in the poor and oppressed in the same unjust situation as before is not reconciliation but passive acquiescence that does not lead to transformation. It is a sad commentary in America that the poor and oppressed are left to reconcile to hopelessness and powerlessness. There is no doubt changes have been made within the system of power by allowing a few from the disadvantaged group to participate in power, but a few do not solve the problem of the many. Unless the socioeconomic structures are corrected so that the disadvantaged group receives justice from past grievances and can make decisions that control their destiny, reconciliation is not real. Anything less than this is unacceptable reconciliation. No one serious about real reconciliation should waste their time engaging in unrealistic reconciliation.

The cost of reconciliation won't be cheap for a nation that held people in slavery for centuries. When the Israelites left Egypt, they had gold and silver as payment for their long centuries in bondage. Black people in America have not been compensated at all, and this has created a generational wealth deficit that has lasted for two and a half centuries. Many people may get upset with this socioeconomic factual diagnosis. However, my question is, would you get upset with your doctor who has made a medical diagnosis that you have cancer or a disease that could kill you? You may not like the news from the doctor, but after careful analysis, second and third opinions, and you indeed have what the doctor said you have, you normally work

---

7. Rosemary Ruether, *Holy Land Hollow Jubilee: God, Justice and the Palestinians* (London: Melisende Publishing LTD, 1999), 121.

with the doctor to save your life. Your healing is contingent upon your cooperation. So it is with the life and soul of the nation. America must hear the truth and work with one another to correct this historical wrong. Reparations are due to black people because it cost them their livelihood, generational wealth, and being able to compete with other groups.

To those who disagree with the cost as part of the reconciliation process, then look at what it costs God to reconcile humanity back to Himself. Jesus Christ gave up His glory, honor, majesty, wealth, and power and lowered Himself to come to earth to save humanity. It cost God the life of His Son to reconcile humanity to God. Dietrich Bonhoeffer stated, "Above all, it is costly because it cost God the life of his Son: "Ye were bought at a price," and what has cost much cannot be cheap for us. Above all, it is grace because God did not reckon his Son too dear a price to pay for our life but delivered him up for us. Costly grace is the Incarnation of God."[8] Is America willing to pay the cost of reconciliation? The jury is still out on this question.

---

8. Dietrich Bonhoeffer, *The Cost of Discipleship* (New York: Macmillion Publishers, 1963), 48.

Chapter Eight

THERMOSTAT CITIZENS

You've got to be a thermostat rather than a thermometer. A thermostat shapes the climate of opinion; a thermometer just reflects it. —CORNEL WEST

The problems we face as a nation and world cannot be solved by ignoring them and by being a thermometer that only registers them. What is needed today are thermostat citizens who are dissatisfied with the problems of this nation and willing to struggle and sacrifice to set the nation on a more just and humane course. Thermostat citizens are needed to change the socioeconomic and political landscape of America because if the nation remains on its current trajectory, it will lead to the death of this great republic. Jesus said, "Every kingdom divided against itself will be ruined, and every city or household divided against itself will not stand (Matthew 12:25)." Americans have a choice to either put conscience over consensus, people over party, Christ over culture, and help save our nation or go along to get along and let the nation topple. Our social, economic, political, and cultural differences are so profound, that American citizens have become a threat to their national security. Unless America comes together and finds common ground, democracy may end up being referred to in past tense terms.

Many citizens are saying it's a leadership problem, the reason America is on a downward spiral. It is believed many leaders have lost touch with the people and the foundational values and principles that initially formed this great republic. Because many of our leaders have lost touch with the people and with God, our nation is worse off. Nationally and internationally we are in a mess, and there is no doubt we have a leadership crisis in America. We have leaders hiding behind systems that reinforce inequality and the status quo. They walk a tightrope trying to address the particular needs of people and, at the same time, not offend those who hold their employment within their power. Leaders find themselves as thermometers pressured to put the political party ahead of the needs of the people. These leaders are discouraged from being thermostats who could set the moral vision, spiritual standards, and political agenda for betterment and progress in America. They are swayed to remain thermometers by the hostile winds of religious, political, and economic power plays of opposition. We don't have enough leaders who are willing to stand amid committing political suicide, losing pulpits, and being fired as CEO to be the moral conscience of the nation. Many of them are tossed here and there like a tumbleweed blowing in the wind of everyone's opinions! Vanity has taken grip of their souls, and we are worse off as a nation because of it. Thermometer leaders are not helping but hurting the nation and its future generations. Alexander Hamilton once said, "If you don't stand for something, you will fall for anything."[1] It is far past the time for thermometer leaders who just register the temperature of society. If we are to emerge better out of our national crisis, we need thermostat leaders who are not afraid to regulate and set the temperature of society.

The national situation we are in is not only the fault of political leaders but also the United States citizenry. Our political, religious, and civic leaders are a reflection of their constituency. Citizens may not be responsible for legislating public policy, but we are called to influence public policy. We are called to speak truth to power. We are called to lift our voices against evil and injustice. Citizens who vote and put leaders in office should place demands on them, and if leaders fail to deliver, they should be held accountable. Likewise, when citizens are ill-informed about issues, their elected leaders should be bold enough to take a stand for what is right.

For example, one cannot help but admire the courage of Liz Cheney and nine other congressional leaders who voted to impeach the former

---

1. A quote attributed to Alexander Hamilton, one of the Founding Fathers.

President for inciting an insurrection in the United States Capitol. Liz Cheney was up for re-election but stood up for what she believed to be a bad and dangerous precedent for the nation. We may not agree with her political philosophy, but we must admire the stand she took to send a message that the actions of January 6, 2021, are dangerous and non-progressive for America. It cost her re-election but history will look back and give her homage for the stand she took to help redirect the dangerous trajectory this nation is on. Liz Cheney made this bold statement:

> We are confronting a domestic threat that we have never faced before—and that is a former President who is attempting to unravel the foundations of our constitutional Republic. He is aided by Republican leaders and elected officials who have made themselves willing hostages to this dangerous and irrational man . . . We're in a situation where former President Trump has betrayed the patriotism of millions and millions of people across our country. Many people here in Wyoming, and he's lied to them . . . And what I know to do is to tell the truth and to make sure that people understand the truth about what happened and why it matters so much . . . No House seat, no office in this land, is more important than the principles that we are all sworn to protect. And I well understood the potential political consequences of abiding by my duty.[2]

Whether one agrees with Cheney or not, the point is she took a stand when she knew it was going to cost her dearly. To be thermostat citizens, we must take a stand even when we know it will cost us dearly.

It is not easy going against the grain of majority opinion, but the future of America hinges on thermostat citizens. We can get inspiration and encouragement from thermostat people in history, and since history is fluid, our act of courage can be included as we help change a nation and world for the betterment of mankind. Who can forget ancient thermostat figures like Moses, who worked for the freedom of his people and promoted the idea of freedom for all mankind? Who can forget the young Jewish men Shadrach, Meshach, and Abednego, who, at the order of the King, refused

---

2. Liz Cheney, "How Liz Cheney Lost Wyoming's Lone Seat In the House," by Eric Bradner and Jeff Zeleny, CNN, August 17, 2022.

to bow before a golden image? Who can forget modern thermostat leaders like Martin Luther, the protestant leader of the Reformation who nailed his ninety-five theses on the door of Wittenberg, influenced significant changes in the Catholic Church, paving the way for Protestantism. Thermostat leader, Mahatma Gandhi practiced civil disobedience in light of unjust laws and brought change for the nation of India. Abraham Lincoln, who declared, "Our nation cannot survive half slave and half free, changed America and brought it closer to its democratic creed. Other people like Frederick Douglass, Ida B. Wells-Barnett, Susan B. Anthony, Rosa Parks, Martin Luther King, Jr., Malcolm X, Ella Baker, and Fannie Lou Hamer were all thermostat voices and activists against what was and is wrong in our nation, and a result brought about significant changes in America and the world. This list of thermostat citizens is by no means exhaustive. There are countless others who, because of their deep convictions and willingness to undergo opposition, abuse, misunderstanding, and suffering, influenced social, cultural, political, and technological changes.

Now more than ever, we need thermostat citizens in every sphere of our nation to set the temperature of love, justice, peace, equality, and unity.

The best unsung thermostat underpaid citizens who are critical in developing thermostat citizens are teachers. Teachers are the ones who shape and form the minds of young people by teaching them how to think and often think outside the proverbial box of conformity. To save America, we must have thermostat teachers in public, private, and religious institutions who can produce thermostat students who can go on and become thermostat citizens, leaders, statesmen, presidents, CEOs, entrepreneurs, etc. Teachers are critical to the transformation of the nation. They are the behind-the-scenes producers of thermostat citizens of a nation. Vartan Gregorian, the 12th president of the Carnegie Corporation of New York, agrees, "Andrew Carnegie, our founder, had an extraordinary vision for our society. He believed in the necessity and the transformational power of education. He also believed that the success of our democracy depends on the quality of our education and of our teachers. Reason and education, he believed, are bedrocks providing not only inspiration but also solutions and engines of progress for our free society. He was a firm believer in our democracy, its institutions, and our Constitution. He was convinced that an educated citizenry was the best guardian of our democracy because they had learned that along with all of the rights bestowed upon them came an obligation to become engaged citizens."[3]

There is no doubt that the health and future of our democracy rest largely with thermostat teachers who understand the condition of our nation and how they can use the classroom to inculcate students with critical thinking and problem-solving abilities to become thermostat citizens to transform our nation for the better. Although teachers are unsung heroes and receive a lot of unwarranted criticism, we cannot change the trajectory of our country without them. As water is essential for the growth of trees teachers are essential for the health of the nation. Justin Belt made a very cogent point:

> The time has come for our buildings to be led by faculty and staff who are thermostats. While the onus is often placed on the Administration to make the proper changes, because they have the overarching views that are necessary, I would argue that from a bottom-to-top method, it has to start with teachers. Teachers have their hands on the students. We are in the hallways and cafeterias. We have hands in seeing discipline issues as they happen, and are often involved in the corrections thereof. If all of this is true, then why should we not embrace the power that comes with setting culture? Why shouldn't our classrooms be microcosms of what our school should be? And why shouldn't our schools be microcosms of what our district and societies could be? The power lies in the small, intentional changes. Whether high-fiving students in the hallway or opening class with culture and community-building activities like welcome circles, each thing that happens with the goal of establishing a mindful, self-aware, and bonded community of learners serves to establish a new temperature. What we also have to consider is that every action establishes a new culture . . . Teachers, optimization is always within grasp so long as we set our hearts, minds, and actions toward leading well.[4]

Not only teachers but everyone of us in all professions must involve ourselves in one way or another to steer our republic away from the dangerous cliff it is about to go over. The temperature of our nation has created a

3. Vartan Gregorian, "Teachers Create the Future of America," *Carnegie Reporter* Spring, April 30, 2021.
4. Justin Belt, "Leadership Lessons: Thermostat vs Thermometer," *Teachers on Fire Magazine*, June 10, 2019.

climate of political division, community strife, racial hatred, anger, bitterness, outright violence, and mayhem. Temperature is extremely important. It is important for our existence; it is important for the food we eat. If food doesn't keep the right temperature, it will spoil and be unfit to eat. Temperature is important for the health of our bodies, the homes we live in, the cars we drive, and the places where we work. Not having the right temperature could mean death to any living organism and can cause inorganic things to malfunction when the temperature is not right.

The temperature in America is too high in toxicity and injustice and too low in justice and humanity. To change the temperature of our nation, we must become thermostat citizens to set the moral temperature of love, justice, equality and humanity to produce a climate different from the one we are living in today. When enough of us become thermostats citizens then "Nothing can stop the power of a committed and determined people to make a difference in our society. Why? Because human beings are the most dynamic link to the divine on this planet."[5] We all represent one drop of water, but when we come together, we are a mighty ocean that can send waves of hope across the world. The question is, which one are we? Thermometers that only reflect the climate around us or thermostats capable of setting the temperature to create a different climate. We must answer this question for ourselves before it is too late. America needs more thermostat citizens who are not afraid to stand and say with the young ancient Hebrews of Babylonian, "O Nebuchadnezzar, we do not need to defend ourselves before you. If we are thrown into the blazing furnace, the God whom we serve is able to save us. He will rescue us from your power, Your Majesty. But even if he doesn't, we want to make it clear to you, Your Majesty, that we will never serve your gods or worship the gold statue you have set up Daniel 3:16-28)" We need more citizens to stand and say with Peter in the early Christian movement, "We ought to obey God rather than men (Acts 5:29)." Think what kind of nation we would have if we had enough leaders in the government, the church, community, schools, institutions, and industries who were thermostats rather than thermometers.

---

5. John Lewis, *Across That Bridge: A Vision For Change and the Future of America* (New York: Hachette Books, 2017), 7.

Conclusion

ANTS AND WHAT WE CAN LEARN FROM THEM

Go to the ant, you sluggard; consider its ways and be wise!
—Proverbs 6:6

When I see all the division in our land, in government, in society, in communities, and in the postmodern church, we would do well to look again at examples of unification. America has lost her way. Instead of being the United States of America, we have become the Divided States of America. The division is very acute and it is being played out across the nation, and we are worse off for it. We have a choice. Either we see our common good and start our way back towards being one nation, under God, indivisible, with liberty, and justice for all or experience the same fate of the decline and fall of the Roman Empire. We can disagree, but we don't have to be disagreeable to the point that we lose our purpose and our sense of nationhood. Two major things destroy a nation: injustice and disunity. If we cannot come together to solve these two major problems, we will not survive as a republic. Jesus said, "Every kingdom divided against itself will be ruined, and every city or household divided against itself will not stand (Matthew 12:25)."

Consistent division is dangerous to a nation. We can disagree over policy but when our core values and principles that serve as a foundation for the nation are ignored, the division is destructive for the republic. Arnold Toynbee reminds us, "Some twenty-six civilizations have risen upon the face of the earth. Almost all of them have descended into the junk heaps of destruction. The decline and fall of these civilizations were not caused by external invasions but by internal decay. They failed to respond creatively to the challenges impinging upon them."[1] They wouldn't come together to solve their common problems; therefore, they didn't survive, and we see the same parallel running throughout our nation today. Division is causing a meltdown of our social and political institutions, and soon, the economy follows.

Solomon, the wisest king in Israel and the author of Proverbs wants us to observe one of the smallest creatures in our ecosystem to gain wisdom to help guide us back towards what we can accomplish through unity and dedication of purpose. He points to the ant. "Go to the ant, you sluggard; consider its ways and be wise (Proverbs 6:6)!" Solomon is pointing out how laziness and irresponsibility can lead to ruin. Too many Americans have become lazy and irresponsible in maintaining democracy. What we don't pay attention to and ignore can have devastating consequences. Too many in our nation are allowing democracy to be run over roughshod by antidemocratic forces. When we are putting party before people, we do not understand that this is irresponsible, and it supports anti-democratic forces while our founding principles are being violated. To save our democracy, we must put in the work, or otherwise, the work of the opposing forces will defeat democracy. We must remember that democracy is only an ideal that can be replaced with another idea of governance. If we don't come together to work and defend democracy, we cannot complain when it is replaced by something else. Democracy means not only paying attention but defending it against all threats. We cannot win against antidemocratic forces when we are not unified in our efforts. To help bring us together, Solomon says through the annals of time to go to the ant and gain wisdom.

Although we are bigger than ants and our brains are larger than theirs, the Scripture points out how small things can teach us big lessons. There are characteristics of the ant that can make us wise to get us through our crisis

---

1. Martin Luther King, Jr. Speech, "The Three Evils of Society," at the National Conference on New Politics, 1967.

as a nation. It is a known fact that ants work together. They demonstrate teamwork. There are more than 12,000 types of ants all over the world, and they work together to achieve common goals. Regardless of how small or large their colonies are, we find ants cooperating with one another to get a job done. We won't find ants standing on the sideline idle and fighting one another because they are busy working fulfilling their common purpose. When one ant is pulling something large, other ants come to its aid to lift the burden so all can benefit from what is brought in. Ants display a remarkable sense of unity, organization, and cooperation. Ants know through experience they can accomplish more by working together than by working apart. They have a "we" rather than "I" mentality. They are not concerned about titles, positions, and rank. They know what affects one directly affects them all indirectly; they stick together around common interests. They know the power of teamwork.

Another characteristic of the ants is they don't need micromanagers watching over them to get a job done. They are not lazy waiting for someone else to do what they can collectively get done. Ants are disciplined and natural self-starters. They work with persistence, getting things done. No one has to tell them time is running out on a deadline to get them to move. Ants are always moving, working, and doing their job to accomplish their goal. The Bible teaches us "Not to be slothful in business, but fervent in spirit serving the Lord (Romans 12:11)." Ants show on a consistent basis they are not slothful in business or anything else.

Another characteristic of the ants is they are not in short supply. When one ant finds food, he goes and gets others, and before you know it, there are hundreds of ants doing their part to benefit the whole colony. We never see one ant struggling with something while others ants are standing around watching with idleness. There is no such thing as the harvest is plentiful but laborers are few when it comes to ants. Ants have plenty of laborers who work without looking for recognition, without looking to be seen, without expecting favors or have ulterior reasons for what they do. Ants just work; they never go on strike; they never undermine one another because they understand they need each other to benefit the whole.

Another characteristic is ants prepare for the future. Not only do they plan but they execute their plan. They don't sit around talking, pontificating, and making excuses. They don't get caught up in the paralysis of analysis. Ants prepare themselves for the future. They don't consume everything they have because they know winter is coming. Unlike grasshoppers that make no preparation for winter and die out, ants prepare and work for their future, and this is why they have survived for thousands of years.

Another characteristic of the ants is they have a sense of community. They know to protect, teach, and share knowledge with the next generation of ants is everybody's responsibility. They don't put this enormous responsibility on one section of their society; they all pitch in nurturing, teaching, and sharing. They understand that community means everybody matters. Everybody is a piece of the continent, a part of the main. They understand it takes a community to survive, thrive, and develop. It is about being connected and responsible for what happens in the community.

Another characteristic of the ant is they never give up. When they run into a situation or circumstance that impedes their goal, they stay together and use their wisdom to go over the situation, go under the situation, or go around the situation. They never let a situation or circumstance stop their onward march toward victory. The scripture teaches, "Let us not be weary in well doing: for in due season we shall reap, if we faint not." Ants are always planning, strategizing, cooperating, and reaping to show us how we can go about doing the Will of God on earth as it is in heaven. We can gain great wisdom from these small creatures of nature to help us forge a better and sustaining future.

Disagreements don't have to divide us; we can solve our human problems if we come together in unity. If we are going to move our nation from polarization to transformation, we need ant-like characters. If we are going to transform our dark todays into bright tomorrows, we need ant-like characters. If we are going to move the postmodern church from division, racial strife, and complacency to a spiritual movement of brotherhood and sisterhood, we need ant-like characters. If we are going to become the thermostat instead of the thermometer in society, we need ant-like characters.

If we are going to inject love, peace, and justice into the veins of our nation to prevent us from destroying ourselves, we need ant-like characters.

To save our democracy, create a better future for our children, and put our nation on a different trajectory, we need to observe and imitate the ant.

Transformation does not roll in on the wheels of inevitably, but by ant-like character, people can make a tremendous difference through the power of unity. As Americans of different backgrounds, shades, colors, religions, and political differences, let us rise up with ant-like characters to lift our nation out of the quicksand of hopelessness to the solid rock of possibility. We need each other, and together, it is going to take unity to solve our national problems.

BIBLIOGRAPHY

Books

Gerard Baker, *American Breakdown Why We No Longer Trust Our Leaders and Institutions and How We Can Rebuild Confidence*, Hachette Book Group, New York, 2023.

Dietrich Bonhoeffer, The Cost of Discipleship, Collier Books MACMILLAN Publishing Company, New York, 1963.

Ben Carson, *One Nation, What We All Can Do to Save America's Future*, SENTINEL, New York, New York, 2014.

Will & Ariel Durant, *The Lessons of History*, Simon & Schuster Paperbacks, New York, New York, 1968.

Tony Evans, *Kingdom Race Theology God's Answer To Our Racial Crisis*, Moody Publishers, Chicago, 2022.

————, *Oneness Embraced A Kingdom Race Theology For Reconciliation Unity And Justice*, Moody Publisher, Chicago, 2022.

Crystal M. Fleming, *How To Be Less Stupid About Race*, Beacon Press, Boston, 2018.

Jeannine Hill Fletcher, *The Sin of White Supremacy, Christianity, Racism, & Religious Diversity in America*, Orbis Books, Maryknoll, New York, 2017.

Joel Edward Goza, *America's Unholy Ghosts: The Racist Roots of Our Faith and Politics*, Cascade Books, Eugene, Oregon, 2019.

Andrew Hacker, *Two Nations Black And White, Separate, Hostile, Unequal*, Ballantine Books, New York, 1992, 1995.

Martin Luther King, Jr., Strength to Love, Fortress Press: Philadelphia, 1963,

Christopher Lasch, The Revolt of the Elite and the Betrayal of Democracy, W.W. Norton & Company, New York, 1995.

John Lewis, Across That Bridge: A Vision For Change and the Future of America, Hachette Books, New York, 2017.

Erwin W. Lutzer, *When A Nation Forgets God, 7 Lessons We Must Learn From Nazi Germany,* Moody Publishers, Chicago, 2010.

Benjamin E. Mays, Walking Integrity Mentor to Martin Luther King, Jr., Edited by Lawrence Edward Carter Sr., Mercer University Press, Macon, Georgia, 1998.

Kevin Phillips, *American Theocracy The Peril And Politics of Radical Religion, Oil, and Borrowed Money in the 21st Century, Viking, Published by Penguin, New York, New York, 2006.*

Rosemary Ruether, *Holy Land Hollow Jubilee: God, Justice and the Palestinians,* London, Melisende Publisher, 1999.

Charles C. Ryrie, What You Should Know About Social Responsibility, Moody Press, Chicago, 1982.

Thomas M. Shapiro, The Hidden Cost of Being African American: How Wealth Perpetuates Inequality, Oxford University Press, 2004, 204.

Christian Smith, Editor, *Disruptive Religion The Force of Faith in Social Movement Activism,* Routledge Press, New York, 1996.

Jemar Tisby, *The Color of Compromise: The Truth About The American Church's Complicity in Racism,* Zondervan, 2019.

Howard Thurman, *The Search For Common Ground, An Inquiry Into The Basis Of Man's Experience Of Community,* Friends United Press, Richmond, Indiana, 1971.

Cornel West, *Race Matters*, Vintage Books, New York, 1993.

Henry Nelson Wieman, Creative Freedom Vocation of Liberal Religion, New York: The Pilgrim Press, 1982.

Articles

Jen Arnold, "The Vertical and Horizontal Beams" Corpus Christi Catholic Church, The Body of Christ Becoming Disciples, 3/28/2020.

Justin Belt, "Leadership Lessons: Thermostat vs Thermometer," *Teachers on Fire Magazine*, June 10, 2019.

Anton Bosch, "Why Is a Large Segment of the Church Powerless," *Charisma Magazine*, February 2, 2016.

Liz Cheney, "How Liz Cheney Lost Wyoming's Lone Seat In the House, by Eric Bradner and Jeff Zeleny, CNN, August 17, 2022.

Barbara Comito, "2020 Vision: Bear One Another's Burdens," blog.union-gospelmission.org, October 8, 2020.

James Comey, *Politico.com,* by Cristiano Lima, May 23, 2018.

Mahatma Gandhi, "Gandhi and Civil Disobedience" Teach Democracy formerly Constitutional Rights Foundation, 2023.

Vartan Gregorian, "Teachers Create the Future of America," *Carnegie Reporter* Spring, April 30, 2021.

Michael Luttig, "Democracy Is Worth Defending," *The Columns* by Sara Butler, columns.wlu.edu, June 2, 2023.

Shawn McAndrew, "We Need Each Other," Hoffmaninstitute.org, 03/28/22.

John MacArthur, "Bearing One Another's Burdens," January 1, 2010, ligonier.org

Jewel Medley, "Abraham Lincoln Predicted U.S. Downfall by Avarice," *The Thinker*, May 28, 2017.

Kelsey Pelzer, Parade.com, July 18, 2023.

Salem Al Suwaidi, *"Is 'American Exceptionalism' A Myth?, Dialogue & Discourse*, November 4, 2020.

Brookings.edu, "To unite a divided nation, we must tackle both vertical and horizontal inequality," Alice M. Rivlin, Allan Rivlin, and Sheri Rivlin, November 5, 2019.

Brookings, "Why We Need Reparations For Black Americans," Rashawn Ray and Andre M. Perry, April 15, 2020.

National Advisory Commission on Civil Disorder, U. S. Government Printing Office, 1968, 1.

Speeches & Lectures

Jimmy Carter, Nobel Lecture, Oslo, December 10, 2002.

Jane Elliott, *An Unfinished Crusade: An Interview with Jane Elliott,* PBS Frontline, January 1, 2023.

Frederick Douglass, Speech on "Southern Barbarism" in 1886 on the 24th Anniversary of Emancipation, Washington, D. C.

Amanda Gorman, "The Hill We Climb," Inaugural Poem at the Presidential Inauguration, January 22, 2021.

Alexander Hamilton, one of the Founding Fathers.

Robert F. Kennedy, Remarks at the University of Kansas, March 18, 1968.

Lyndon B Johnson, "To Fulfill These Rights," Commencement Address at Howard University, June 4, 1965.

Martin Luther King, Jr., "Facing the Challenge of a New Age," 1956.

———, "Letter From the Birmingham Jail," August, 1963.

———, "I Have A Dream Speech," Lincoln Memorial March on Washington, August 1963.

———, Martin Luther King, Jr. Speech, "The Three Evils of Society," at the National Conference on New Politics, 1967.

———, "The Other America" Grosse Point High School on March 14, 1968.

Abraham Lincoln, "House Divided Speech," Springfield, Illinois, June 16, 1858, Neely, Mark E. Jr. 1982.

———, Speech at Kalamazoo, Michigan, August 27, 1856.

———, Address Before the Young Men's Lyceum of Springfield, January 27, 1838.

Committee on Theological Prospectus, National Committee of Black Churchmen (NCBC), June 13, 1969.

Internet Sources

Frederick Douglass, cited from barteby.com/essay/Summary-of-Frederick-Douglass.

John Dunn, all poetry.com

got questions.org "What does it mean to bear one another's burdens (Galatians 6:2)?"

Preamble to the Declaration of Independence, "America's Founding Documents, archives.gov

Martin Niemoller, "First they came for the Socialists," United States Holocaust Memorial Museum in Washington, D.C. February 5, 2011.

Maya Angelou, brainyquote.com

Shalom, Kate, Kateshopecafe.net, November 11, 2022.

ABOUT THE AUTHOR

Reginald F. Davis is a pastor, scholar, and native of Memphis, Tennessee. He is the author of nine additional books in the field of theology and religion including *Bible Study for Busy Pastors and Ministers and Transforming Faith to Shape the World Around Us*. He has lectured at colleges, universities, and churches across the nation. He holds a Bachelor of Arts from Incarnate Word College, a Masters of Divinity from Colgate Rochester Divinity School, and a Ph.D. from Florida State University.

He lives in Williamsburg, Virginia, with his wife and children.

www.ingramcontent.com/pod-product-compliance
Lightning Source LLC
Chambersburg PA
CBHW010732270326
41934CB00016B/3459